PENGUIN BOOKS

During his storied 36-fight career, Tyson Fury has established himself as one of the best heavyweight fighters of all time.

Born and raised in Manchester, Fury weighed just 1lb at birth after being born three months premature. His father John named him after Mike Tyson.

From Irish Traveller heritage, the 'Gypsy King' first shocked the boxing world in 2015, when he stunned long-time champion Wladimir Klitschko to win the WBA, IBF and WBO world heavyweight titles.

Due to struggles with his mental health, Tyson did not fight again for more than two years. Most thought he was done with boxing forever, until an amazing comeback fight with Deontay Wilder in December 2018. It was an instant classic, ending in a split-decision tie. Tyson was victorious in the second fight against Deontay Wilder in February 2020, defeating his opponent by seventh-round technical knockout. In October 2021, Tyson concluded the trilogy with victory against Deontay Wilder by an emphatic eleventh-round technical knockout. In March 2022, Fury successfully defended his heavyweight crown at Wembley Stadium against Dillian Whyte, winning by knockout with a devastating uppercut in the sixth round.

Outside of the ring, Tyson Fury is a mental health ambassador. He lives with his wife Paris and seven children in Morecambe, and most mornings can be found running and training along Morecambe Bay.

This book was first published in November 2022 and does not span boxing events that have occurred since then.

Also by Tyson Fury

Behind the Mask
The Furious Method

TYSON FURY

GLOVES OFF

PENGUIN BOOKS

PENGUIN BOOKS

UK | USA | Canada | Ireland | Australia
India | New Zealand | South Africa

Penguin Books is part of the Penguin Random House group of companies
whose addresses can be found at global.penguinrandomhouse.com

First published by Century in 2022
Published in Penguin Books 2024

001

Copyright © Tyson Fury, 2022

The moral right of the author has been asserted

Typeset in 13.35/17.13 pt Perpetua MT Std by Jouve (UK), Milton Keynes
Printed and bound in Great Britain by Clays Ltd, Elcograf S.p.A.

The authorised representative in the EEA is Penguin Random House Ireland,
Morrison Chambers, 32 Nassau Street, Dublin D02 YH68

A CIP catalogue record for this book is available from the British Library

ISBN: 978–1–804–94157–7

www.greenpenguin.co.uk

Penguin Random House is committed to a
sustainable future for our business, our readers
and our planet. This book is made from Forest
Stewardship Council® certified paper.

This book is dedicated to anyone with mental health problems. Know this: there is hope and nothing is impossible. If I could make my comeback, so can you.

Warning: sensitive content. This book contains depictions of a suicide attempt and suicidal thoughts and may be troubling and triggering for some readers. If you have been affected by mental health problems and have experienced or are experiencing suicidal thoughts please get professional help immediately — a list of mental health resources are available at the end of this book. This book draws on my personal experiences, and I hope you may find some of my approaches to mental health useful. But what works for me will not work for everyone and I am not an expert, so you may require medication and medical help.

The author and publishers disclaim, as far as the law allows, any liability arising directly from the use or misuse of the information contained in this book.

CONTENTS

Introduction: The Legend of
The Gypsy King   1

PART ONE: THE UNDEFEATED

1. Spilled Blood   13
2. No Guts, No Glory   25
3. Let's Fight   39
4. Family Guy   59
5. End Game   79
6. The U-Turn   93
7. It's Not All Sunshine and Rainbows   107
8. Lionheart   121

PART TWO: ANGELS AND DEMONS

9. Son   139
10. The Right Side of the Tracks   155
11. First Blood   169
12. To the Moon   187
13. I Hate Myself and I Want to Die   201
14. 1,000 Days   221
15. The Second Coming   235
16. The King of America   249

CONTENTS

17. The Greatest Showman   263
18. New Day Rising   277

    Mental Health Contacts & Helplines   293
    Professional Boxing Record   297
    Index   303
    List of Illustrations   315

GLOVES OFF

THE LEGEND OF THE GYPSY KING

23 April 2022. Wembley Stadium. *Fury v Whyte*.

It was show time, dossers.

And the arena went crazy. Lights and camera flashes flickered around the crowd. Lads threw pints; women screamed my name. And who could blame them? This was a showdown for the history books, a bout against the British heavyweight, Dillian 'The Body Snatcher' Whyte at a rammo Wembley Stadium heaving with 94,000 punters – the biggest ever crowd for a European boxing match. After two years of pandemic misery, the country was thirsty for a massive party and The Gypsy King was going to give them one. The hype had been so big that ticket sales for *Fury v Whyte* outsold some of the most famous names in pop music.

Making an entrance to remember on a night like this was a big deal, so I was carried into the arena on a gold throne. And as I was hoisted into the air, I felt like a master of the universe; this is the superstar atmosphere I've always enjoyed as a boxer and the experience of connecting with it has always been surreal and incredible. At that moment, I became super-charged, like I'd been plugged into the electrics and my adrenaline soared. *Not bad for an old, fat fella*, I thought, looking around at the craziness. *A bald-headed lad from Morecambe, a seaside town in the middle of nowhere* . . . But even though I was partying too, my eyes were still fixed on the prize. I needed a win to match the pizzazz.

I'd picked a soundtrack to match the mood and it rocked through the Wembley PA. The first cut was 'Sex on Fire' by Kings of Leon – a song that had often helped me to find a groove in training. I belted it out with everyone in the stadium, like we were pals in a karaoke pub, or celebrating an England win in the World Cup. The second song, 'Juicy' by rapper The Notorious B.I.G. (AKA Biggie Smalls), was there because its lyrics – *It was all a dream* – reminded me of my own life. Being Tyson Fury *was* like a dream. In Biggie's case, he'd read hip-hop magazines as a kid, listened to rap radio and stuck pictures of his heroes to the bedroom wall before becoming a legend. I'd been the same, but with boxing. I'd watched the fights, read about the great heavyweights and tacked photos of my heroes around the place. Some people told me I wouldn't make it as a fighter and the same had been said to Biggie about his music career, but neither of us had listened to the critics, we'd both reached for the stars instead. And tonight, I was ready to shine.

The crowd seemed to whirl around me like leaves in a hurricane, and I was the eye. As the noise for my final entrance continued to build, I knew that these were my people and this was my moment. The nine-year-old version of myself would have loved the buzz and the colour. *So soak up every second of it, pal,* I thought. And when I saw the ring ahead it was hard not to think about what would happen to the boxing world once I'd left. *Who could fill this void?* At that point, retirement was on my mind and about to become a major talking point, but if I walked away for good, the sport would probably return to how it was, pre-Gypsy King, full of boring fighters that very few people cared about. The papers were going to miss me too. I only had to crack open a can of lager, or walk into a pub with my shirt off for them to write a front-page headline.

These were the nights I lived for. I was like a gladiator striding into his arena and it was hard not to feel a sense of pride because my contest with Whyte seemed like so much more than a boxing match. That had a lot to do with the date: 23 April, St George's Day, a moment in the calendar that means a lot to me because I'm very proud of my roots. *Fury v Whyte* was an all-English clash too, a moment in national sporting history and you know how us English do when it comes to a battle: we hold our shit down. Psychologically, the fact that I was fighting on home turf for the first time in years was a motivational boost. It was a death or glory clash and I wanted to do everything in my power to bring a buzz to the nation.

For this momentous occasion I was wearing a white and red robe, England colours. I'd also heard a person could look much bigger than they actually were when dressed in white, thanks to a trick of the eye. (In much the same way that wearing black creates a slimming effect.) To my opponent I must have looked humungous, like a 6 foot 9 monster. And terrifying, because I'd picked a pair of specially designed St George's Cross boxing gloves for the battle. *A fist wrapped in a flag.* My plan was to smack Whyte in the mouth so hard that the country would be shaking for days afterwards.

Some people were doubting my chances of winning, but no way was I was messing up at Wembley Stadium, and to make sure I ran through my usual pre-match routines during the build-up. In the dressing room, I moved about in my underpants, singing and dancing, cracking jokes, only stopping to take a seat on the massage table to watch the undercard and have my hands wrapped. I've studied boxers my whole life, as both a fan and a fighter, and knew that before a title bout I was unlike a lot of the others. Stress ricocheted off me, even in a venue as big as Wembley Stadium, and I liked to mess about with the music cranked loud. I've seen many other changing rooms throughout my career and most of them were like death parties. You'd think the boxers involved were going under the guillotine. Blokes were pale and panting; they shook with nerves and punched the walls as a way of firing themselves up. Everyone alongside them looked frazzled with terror.

But not me: not in my space, and definitely not at Wembley. I was a disco diva getting ready to shine; I was about to get paid and about to get laid and I loved having the cameras and the press around me in the dressing room because it added to the sense of occasion. During those moments I could tell what everybody was thinking: *Why is he acting like this? He's going out there to fight a man who could potentially kill him with one punch. He just don't give a damn* . . . But that's what sets me apart from most people in life. Giving a damn is not my thing, and knowing my resolve won't wobble under pressure, I have every confidence my body won't falter either, no matter the challenge. The faith that I can withstand all punishment then creates even more self-belief in what is an ever-expanding circle of positivity. Wembley, though being my biggest ever fight, was no different. I was ready to go.

I ran through a warm-up with my dad John alongside me, plus my trainer SugarHill Steward – a former Detroit policeman and the nephew of the Boxing Hall of Fame trainer, Emanuel 'Manny' Steward – and the nutritionist George Lockhart. Together we moved through some pad work. *Bang! Bang! Bang!* Everything felt nice and easy, though I wasn't overconfident or in a massively cocky mood. I always took precautions and as I got myself together for the walk into Wembley, I pulled my team about me for a group prayer.

'Dear Lord, please give us strength and the ability to go in there and give our best performance,' I said. 'We pray for the opponent to do exactly the same, and most of all, we pray that both men can come out in one piece and go home to their families.'

The time to rock 'n' roll had arrived.

• • •

My boxing life has been made up of two careers. The first took place between 2008 and 2015, a period in which I was unable to recognise the psychological demons dragging me down. They pulled on me like a rucksack full of stones, despite the fact I was on my way to becoming the heavyweight champion of the world. The second career kicked off in 2018 after a brutal battle with my mental health, a war I'm still locked into today. Through sheer will I was able to overcome my issues and return as the planet's most entertaining pugilist.

Most books begin at the beginning and end at the end, which might work for your average, run-of-the-mill author. But The Gypsy King is a bona fide legend and a once in a lifetime superhero, so why on earth would I tell my story in an average, run-of-the-mill way? It's for this reason that

Gloves Off starts at the end, and finishes at the beginning of the end, with my full and uncensored roller coaster of a journey jammed in between – and the revelations will spin your head in the best possible way. I'll tell you about the glories of my second career and discuss the idea that I might leave the stage while still at the peak of my powers. Then I'll detail where I came from and how I defeated the then champion, Wladimir Klitschko, in 2015 to become a boxing Titan, before explaining how I very nearly lost everything. (But I was able to claw it all back.) Yeah, I wrote about depression in my first book *Behind The Mask*, but everything was so raw back then. I was still working through my illness at that time and I've since found a new sense of perspective, in and out of boxing. I'm also at a point where I have a reckoning to contend with: the realisation that my professional adventure is drawing to a close. It's from this perspective that I'll relive several other famous events and fights that I've written about previously. I hope you'll enjoy the new insights and a fresh twist or two.

So while I've long been admiral of HMS *I Don't Give A Crap*, the most entertaining showman since the days of Muhammad Ali and the greatest fighter of my generation, it's important to know that, as far as I'm concerned, boxing has always been a business with a shelf life. A sport, yes, a lucrative form of entertainment, for sure, but statistically the people that stay in the game for too long have a tendency to get damaged, *really damaged*, and I don't want that happening to me.

There's also a risk that my career has been shortened by the way in which I've lived my life. Health and nutrition was not exactly a priority for large chunks of my time as a pro: I ballooned in weight between bouts and then, during the mental health breakdown that started in 2015, I boozed, binged and tried cocaine. There was even an attempt at ending it all a year later when I pointed my Ferrari at a bridge and slammed on the accelerator, though I changed my mind at the last second and pulled away – *thank God*. When I eventually asked for help I was diagnosed as being bipolar, paranoid and suffering from anxiety and obsessive compulsive disorder (OCD). I later recovered, but my mental health issues remain a constant work in progress – from time to time I can have suicidal thoughts, though I now understand what's needed to keep my demons at arm's length.

It's not as if boxing is my entire world either. The reality is that I'm a husband, a dad, a son, a brother, and an uncle. My family are my armour and Paris and my six beautiful kids are always in my thoughts because they're so precious to me. On the eve of my 2021 fight with Deontay Wilder I slept on a hospital floor as our youngest child, Athena fought for her life shortly after being born and her successful battle inspired me to win mine. Three years earlier, it was Paris who picked me off the canvas when I'd been poleaxed by depression. At the beginning of my career, my dad and my uncles provided me with the tools to become a top boxer, though I was also taught how to earn an honest day's wage by selling second-hand cars. Throughout my life, the Fury family has provided all the love and support I've needed to succeed. I want them to receive the same love as me, *from me*.

So while getting my face punched in for a living has put millions of pounds in the bank, a fighter needs to know when their time is up – and mine is near. The issue of whether I will fight again could have been settled by the time you read this book: I might have retired, knocked out another dosser or perhaps agreed to a bout in the near future (and the speculation surrounding that decision has been a right circus). In this book I want you to know the truth about my thinking regarding these decisions. A lot's been going through my head, and me changing my mind lately isn't a flippant thing. Walking away from boxing may be the hardest thing I ever do. All I know is that I don't want to overstay my welcome, ruin my legacy, or die from a big right to the side of the head. And believe me, an ending like that has felt worryingly real at times. I even experienced short-term memory loss following that bruising encounter with Wilder in 2021, when, in the hours after the win, my head covered in tennis ball-sized lumps, it was impossible to remember how many times I'd gone down. Everything was foggy, and the experience frightened me. No way do I want to end up living out my days in a wheelchair, or eating my dinners through a straw.

So here it all is for the first time: my boxing life set out in full, from the first fight to (maybe) the last, the highs and the lows, and all the hits and knockdowns in between. Over the coming pages I'll dish out stories and secrets; I'll tell you about my toughest adversaries in and out of the ring, and lay out the reasons for why I'll eventually walk away from professional boxing in my prime, as a legend. Believe me, no other boxing story can lay a glove on this one.

So what are you waiting for?

Get stuck in!

Tyson Fury, Morecambe Bay, September 2022

PART ONE

The Undefeated

CHAPTER ONE

SPILLED BLOOD

Here's what was going through my mind at the end of 2021. I was tired of boxing. *Sick of it*. I'd well and truly had enough and the thought of retiring was becoming more and more appealing. It hadn't been an overnight brainwave though, or a kneejerk reaction. Instead, the idea had been building for a while, over a period of time and a number of hits to the head and body. But despite my feelings, I still wanted to consider the implications long and bloody hard because walking away from the sport I'd once loved for so long wasn't an easy thing to do.

The bottom line was this: at the time I was thirty-three years old and the feeling that I might have been getting on a bit was playing on my mind. Some people could have argued that, at my age, I was still in my prime as a heavy-weight; I suppose ordinarily that would have been the case, but one of the things I'd learned from studying boxing was that too many people struggled to recognise when their time was up. For one reason or another, they couldn't walk away and in the end they hung around for so long that their decision eventually came back to bite them on the arse. I'm talking about the fighters that didn't pay enough attention to their game, or couldn't recognise their breaking points. Rather than listening to their bodies, or the subtle warnings their brains were sending them, they pressed ahead. Perhaps they'd chosen to ignore the alarm bells because they were in denial, or had become too obsessed with money and fame. Having carried on for too long – taking on one last match, maybe ten – they then tarnished their record by losing a lot of blood in the battle, destroying what might have been an incredible legacy. No way was I following that path. I was the best fighter in the game at the time. What I'd achieved was more valuable than a massive bank account, or the satisfaction of seeing my face on the telly.

I even watched Wladimir Klitschko refuse to accept his truth close up when I came to fight him in 2015. He was thirty-nine years old and clearly slowing down, even though he was still the reigning champion. For some reason, he couldn't see his end was on the horizon, but I could. So I told him.

'Every dog has its day,' I said. 'The mind might be willing but the body won't follow.'

He wasn't having it. 'Age is just a number, it's how you feel.'

I shook my head. 'You'll find out that's not true. At the end of the day, you've been a great world champion, but boxing's a young man's game.'

I proved my point shortly afterwards, beating him in the Esprit Arena in Düsseldorf after a full twelve rounds and a unanimous decision to take the WBA (Super), IBF, WBO, IBO and *Ring* titles for the first time. So I knew that there was no way of cheating time; what had happened to Klitschko could just as easily happen to me if I wasn't careful, and a few years after my 2018 comeback, I found myself weighing up my options. I realised there was nothing to be gained by overstaying my welcome like an unwanted party guest.

Losing was one thing, but the risk to my mortality was a whole other ball game, and so far I'd avoided any serious injuries. That said, I was experiencing pain on a daily basis. The wear and tear on my body was becoming noticeable, mainly in my elbows and shoulders, but that was hardly surprising given I'd banged, punched and ripped at things for a living. Most of the time I gritted my teeth through the discomfort and whenever that got too much I'd see a doctor. Still, I understood there was a chance my luck would run out at some point and that I'd injure myself in such a way that I would be screwed up for the rest of my life. A serious back or hand injury didn't bear thinking about, though the more extreme consequences of violence were much nastier, like a bomb to the side of the head that could kill or paralyse me. There was no way I wanted to put my family through that ordeal, especially Paris, because she would be the one left to push me around for the rest of my days. Those risks had to be taken seriously.

There was also the understanding that my career had affected everyone around me, from the minute I'd turned pro. Mum never watched me fight; she hated it. Paris turned as white as a sheet whenever I took a punch; she hated it too. While the kids had grown up knowing all about my career and loved me being in the limelight, they didn't like it when another fighter laid a glove on me; I was an *Invincible* to them. Of course, I had a different perspective. (Well, I would.) Whenever I was fighting, only the heavyweight world championship was on the line and I didn't give much thought to anything else because I knew I was going to win. But for the family as a whole, the stakes were so much higher. My making it through a fight unhurt was their world and they used to stress that everything might come crashing down were I to mess up in some way. It was time to take that stress into consideration.

That's why boxing is such a selfish profession and boxers are such selfish people. A fighter risks his or her health alone. That means they have to think about themselves a lot of the time. And if you think I'm chatting bollocks, take a look at the fans screaming and yelling at the men or women in the ring the next time you're watching a fight in a rowdy stadium or pub. You think *they'd* want to take a punch or ten? The only person that can take those blows, or throw those shots back, is the person in the battle. So don't be surprised when that person then dedicates every hour of their day to being the best, because the reality is that if they don't, there's a good chance their next opponent will cause them some serious damage. That's the reason why any fighter worth their salt makes everything about them during the build-up to a big fight, even if it means living away from home in a training camp for two to three months at a time. They have to be a selfish motherfucker. The chances of them being a success are slim otherwise, no matter how many amazing trainers, nutrition experts or advisers they have about the place.

That is exactly my attitude. During training camps, I am like a Spartan warrior. It doesn't matter whether I'm preparing to fight one bloke or an army, I'm going to do everything to win, my opponents are losing, and I'm not going to let anybody distract me as I work. Everything is blocked out; life's petty matters have to wait until the fight is over. I don't want to know about any news until the right time has arrived, and at the start of every camp I set out the rules: 'I can't be hearing about day-to-day life. I don't want to know about what happened at the supermarket. I don't want to know that someone's been to the dentist. Tell me about it after the fight.'

Like I said, boxing's a selfish sport. I have to live in a different world.

Paris was OK with that attitude because life had always been that way for us, ever since we'd been kids. I'd always boxed and she'd always understood that I had to become a different person in training camp. I couldn't be in Husband Mode; I couldn't be in Daddy Mode; or Brother, Son, or Friend Mode, for that matter. I had to be in Fight Mode because so much was on the line, but there was no doubt it had been a massive sacrifice for everyone. Throughout my career I've been away from my family for long periods of time, whether that was by being on the road, travelling or training, so coming home was another reason to consider retirement – I owed it to everyone I loved.

None of these motives for retiring should be mistaken for fear by the way. I certainly don't feel scared for myself; it's the people around me I worry for. I've never been intimidated by an opponent and I've always stepped into the ring knowing I'm going to smash the other fella to bits, whatever happens. In fact, around the time I first considered leaving the sport, I took the kids to a fairground. As we walked past the stalls and through the arcades, I saw a punch ball machine. A picture of my face glowed on the front in bright lights and underneath, in big letters, was something I'd said in a press conference a few years previously:

I'm not even scared of the devil. If the devil confronted me, I'd confront him as well.

That line pretty much sums up my attitude. I stare down the devil every day, especially when I am dealing with life's distractions and temptations, though that only really happens when I haven't been in the gym for a while, or if my routine is thrown out of kilter. My dad thinks I'm weird; as do my cousins and brothers. The other day, Dad said to me: 'You've achieved everything. You're a multimillionaire. And the best thing you can think of in life is to go to the gym twice a day? You need your head testing.' But that's what makes me happy; not exercising makes me sad. So I went for a run to feel better about it all and my dad, brother and cousin 'kidnapped' me. They took me for a drive that ended up with them dragging me to all these places that were supposed to be fun, but actually turned out to be non-existent rubbish. It took me away from the house and out of my routine at a time when I wanted to be moving from errand to errand. By the time I'd finished running around with them like a headless chicken I felt thoroughly depressed. It messed my day up because I don't like being idle. I want to get up at the crack of dawn and work, not stopping until I've closed my eyes at night.

In those situations, if ever I do feel bad, I think back to the country song, 'I'm Gonna Have a Little Talk With Jesus' by Randy Travis. In the lyrics, the devil tries to drag Randy into a dark spot. The singer even speaks about seeing his face a hundred times, and to get over it, he checks in with Jesus at the end of the day. I've decided that's what I'll do too, because my belief is that before anyone does anything in life, good or bad, there is a get-out moment. A split second of opportunity where they can either fall prey to the temptation in front of them, or regain some composure and move on. It's down to the individual to know how to stand strong, but it requires a healthy state of mind to succeed. I want to do everything possible to be emotionally ready for these moments. That way I can make the right call whenever the devil comes around.

So considering my daily showdowns, what makes you think I'd be afraid of a boxing match?

● ● ●

There was another reason to think about quitting while I was still ahead: I'd watched too many of my heroes retiring badly.

The clichéd backstory of a boxer speaks of someone without a lot of brains, certainly someone who hasn't come from an educated, or privileged background. Instead they've scrapped their way out of the roughest part of town before being put on the right path in the boxing gym. If they are talented enough, they're immediately thrust into the limelight and introduced to a crazy new world as a pro. *It's sink or swim time.* But despite their talents, they don't have any experience with money. They don't have any experience with business. They don't have any experience of lawyers or managers, agents or the taxman. *And why would they?* Everything is alien and so they sink, making bad decision after bad decision – regardless of whether they're any good in the ring or not – before inevitably running out of cash. Forced to stay in the game so they can retire with something, *anything,* in their bank account, they are then battered from pillar to post. And still they end up poor.

Of course, there were exceptions to the rule. Larry Holmes was reported to have opened a series of businesses following his departure from the sport – his portfolio included a nightclub, some restaurants, a training facility and business complex. George Foreman came out of retirement and then made a second career for himself by promoting the George Foreman Grill. That made him a few quid, and then some. Lennox Lewis held on to his money too. But there were thousands more fighters that finished up flat out broke than rich.

I'm not heading that way because my dad has long taught me that the key to avoiding the financial banana skins is to surround yourself with a strong and supportive team. I was also raised to be straight and honest, like a nail. If I bought something at a price, I stood on, no matter how screwed up it later turned out to be. I had to be a man of my word. What I said, I did, and if I didn't deliver on my promises, then I was a piece of shit.

I had cash as a kid, because I was taught how to earn from an early age (we'll get on to that later), and so the upbringing I experienced has made me very different to a lot of fighters. Image isn't my thing either. (Though don't get me wrong, I know my value and I love to put on a show – it just isn't the be all and end all.) I don't like throwing my earnings around like nobody's business either. Yeah, I'm guilty of splashing a few quid here and there, and at the top of my list is a Rolls-Royce Jeep, but I also own a £700 VW Passat, which gets way more miles because I use it as a run-around every day. No lie, I find more enjoyment in the Passat than the Rolls because no one cares about a bloke in a Passat. They don't stare. They don't point. And they don't ask for pictures. But whenever I swan about town in the Roller I never get five minutes of peace.

So at the end of 2021, as I was weighing all of this up, I felt there was nothing to be gained from hanging around in the game for too long. It helped that I'd already earned enough money and been smart with it. In boxing terms I'd also gone beyond what I'd thought was possible, times a million. I felt happy with who I was at the beginning of my career. I felt happy with who I was as I approached the end. Forget risking my rep by fighting into my late thirties, or longer. There was too much at stake.

Some fighters found the fame and fortune too hard to walk away from. Not me. I also knew that the minute other fighters had made their retirement official, public demand had often made them think otherwise. This is one of the reasons why boxing is such a hard sport to say goodbye to; there will always be someone who wants a retiring fighter to hang on for longer, especially if they're at the peak of their powers. Still, I wasn't going to risk losing a few fights, or hitting the skids.

'Why should anyone else get to say when enough is enough?' I thought. 'And if I leave it to someone else to pick my end date, when will that be? Two more years? Six more years? One more fight? *One more fight after one more fight?*'

So if I decided to continue it would be on my terms, because every career had to come to an end eventually and I wanted mine to conclude right. I'd given my blood to boxing for twenty years as both an amateur and pro. There wasn't too much more to spill.

CHAPTER TWO

NO GUTS, NO GLORY

If one fight showed me how dangerous boxing could really be, it was my third and final battle with the American, Deontay Wilder in 2021. I emerged victorious, but bloody hell, it was a slog. I can remember taking so many powerful hits to the head that even the simple act of thinking straight became a mission once the contest was finished. Afterwards I told Paris I'd made up my mind. I was done.

'This is the last one, baby. I won't put you through no more—'

'Thank God for that,' she said.

The only other person I needed to speak to on the matter was my promoter, Frank Warren. I didn't make a big deal out of it. I just gave him the news, straight.

'Look, I'm retiring after the fight.' I said.

Fair play to him, Frank didn't try to change my mind. 'Whatever you want to do, it's your choice,' he said. 'If you want to carry on with boxing, then great; if you don't, also great. You've got to do what's best for you . . .'

I felt good about my decision. The important people in my life had been told, and with Deontay Wilder packed off to bed I was going to live a life of comfort, having made more than enough money. Plus Paris and I had just had our sixth child, Athena. The future life of The Gypsy King was all mapped out. But as a certain someone once said: *Everyone has a plan until they get punched in the mouth.*

Turns out I was no different.

• • •

Let's go back a little bit.

Each and every one of my three fights with Deontay Wilder between 2018 and 2021 was a battle, and understandably so because the bloke was a beast. As the reigning WBC world heavyweight champion, he was built like a brick shithouse, a 6 foot 7 high wall of muscle, tattoos and rage. Wilder also had no clues when it came to tasting defeat – he was an absolute badass with a 40–0 record. Nobody in their right mind wanted to fight him at the time. Well, nobody apart from me.

'Sod it,' I thought, when the fight was arranged. 'I'll lose some weight and get in there. Then I'll beat him up and knock him out.'

Several months earlier, before the Wilder fight had been set, I'd started the process of shaving away ten stone in weight. Bloody hell, I was a right state. I hadn't exactly looked after my body during the early stages of my career and as a young pro, I would often train and then shove a load of pies down my gullet. That process only worsened during my horrific breakdown, where I drank way too much and binged on junk food, expanding to around 30 stone in weight. The recovery was brutal and under the instruction of my new coach, Ben Davison, I hammered myself into the ground to get fit and emotionally well again. For a few months, Ben even moved into the Fury family home and I trained with him every day, twice a day, as I worked on getting back in shape.

While this was going on, the haters arrived in force to shoot their mouths off with claims that I would never return to boxing's top level. *Dumb move*. The talking only fired me up even more: I was the lineal heavyweight champion of the world, so in my head quitting was not an option. One morning I decided to run up the Jubilee Tower, a steep hill in Lancaster. This was a challenge much loved by the local health fanatics with their six packs and Fitbits, but I was still overweight and massively out of puff, and as I made my first few strides a car passed me by.

'Get in the back, mate,' shouted the driver. 'It's too far to the top. You're going to have a heart attack.'

The offer of a lift was like a red rag to a bull. Someone had told me that running up the Jubilee Tower was impossible, so that meant I was bloody well going to do it.

'I'm getting to the bloody mountain top,' I shouted. 'Don't worry about me. And if I have a heart attack, kick me in the nuts while I'm down for being a fat bastard.'

Salvaging my boxing career was also a major project at the time because when I'd withdrawn from the Klitschko rematch in 2016 due to injury, my licence was suspended by the British Boxing Board of Control. In the end my licence was eventually reinstated, and everybody wanted to know who my first big opponent would be. There were two potential names on the wishlist – Anthony Joshua and Deontay Wilder. Though first up I had to win a couple of comeback fights against the Albanian Sefer Seferi in June 2018 and then, a couple of months later, Francesco Pianeta of Germany. Both were dispatched without too much bother and when a hyped fight between Joshua and Wilder failed to materialise, I was given a free shot at the American. A lot of people thought I was taking on too dangerous an opponent, too soon. Ben feared that I hadn't recovered enough, as did my dad, who wouldn't speak to me for several weeks because I'd ignored his warnings that fighting Wilder might kill me. Meanwhile, Wilder probably thought he was on to an easy payday, given the state of me during the last few years.

I couldn't have cared less. My confidence had reached new altitudes and with the fight confirmed for 1 December 2018 in the Staples Center, Los Angeles, I became unshakeable again. Nothing was going to intimidate me and I proved it at the press conference at the BT TV offices in London, where I stated exactly what I was going to do to Wilder. I told him I wanted to feel his punches, before goading him into a body spar; I called him 'a big dosser' as the promoter Frank Warren stood between us. Then, when he eventually gave me a shove, I laughed in his face.

'My wife pushes harder than that!' I shouted.

'Have you ever looked into the eyes of a killer?' he said.

Wilder thought he could rile me up. But he was wrong. 'Plenty of them,' I said. 'And I'm looking at a pussycat. Killers don't dress like you. You're all mouth and no action. All front and no substance. A big hollow shell in a big frame.'

I had a bloody good reason for feeling so strong at the time. I'd decided the fight wasn't just for me; after my experiences with depression, *Fury v Wilder* had become a fight for the millions of people suffering from a mental health issue. I wanted to be a beacon of light for anyone experiencing an emotionally rocky time and knowing I was in the process of overcoming my problems, I reckoned that defeating Wilder – the sport's biggest puncher – would prove to the world that it was possible to heal and succeed. That was some powerful rocket fuel at my back; I felt inspired and talked about my story in interviews, though this new way of thinking was very different to how I'd operated before my last world heavyweight title fight against Klitchsko in 2015.

Back then everything had been about beating the fighter at the top of the tree, nothing more, nothing less.

The Tyson Fury of 2018 was a new prospect. Even though the odds were stacked against me in the Staples Center, I felt no doubts as I walked to the ring, singing and dancing, my tongue wagging. Gala's 1996 house classic, 'Freed From Desire' pulsed through the building. *The Gypsy King was back.* I kissed the wooden crucifix around my neck and bumped fists with the fans. There was a determination to take so much more out of the experience than during my last world title fight, but there was really no other way to think. I had to believe in myself because sometimes that was the only difference between a top-class performer and the person in second place. The winner knows it's his or her time as they step into the moment; they use the pressure to drive themselves forward. But the loser arrives full of fear; they're cowed by uncertainty. I've long understood that if you don't believe a victory is inevitable, there is every chance a loss is coming your way. It's one of the reasons why the men's England football team have blown so many penalty shootouts over the years.

The truth is this: you'll move mountains if you can carry faith the size of a mustard seed. That was my belief and for the first nine rounds against Wilder I was able to prove it because a win seemed to be very much on the cards. I out-fought and out-thought the big dosser, ducking away from his biggest shots and clocking him with a series of heavy hits; I laughed in his face and flicked my tongue out to taunt him. After the first eight rounds, the judges had marked me down as winning a lot of them, and then I got cocky. Following a burst of short rights to my face in the ninth, I allowed Wilder to clip me around the back of the skull and I dropped to the floor. My feeling was that he'd thrown an illegal, behind-the-head punch and should have received a warning from the ref, but no call was made.

Was I bothered? *Nope.* Not getting the decision was hardly surprising. I was in Wilder's backyard; it was his show, his country and his fans. The big shouts were always likely to swing the way of the home fighter because that's what happens in a fight of that nature. In many ways, a contest on foreign soil was a bit like starting a round of golf without a driver. I understood that to win, I would have to do something very special. And if I couldn't and the fight remained relatively tight at the death, the points might not go my way. I got to my feet quickly and loaded up on Wilder again, rocking him with some heavy one-twos before outboxing him in round eleven.

Then came the big plot twist. As I jogged to the corner, my trainer, Ben Davison told me to play it smart. 'You're winning,' he said. 'Don't take risks. See it out . . .'

Ben believed that I was leading on points, which meant

Wilder needed a knockout punch in the final round to snatch victory. Acting rashly, he warned, was going to give it to him on a plate. But I was looking to deliver something much more spectacular than a cautious performance. When the bell dinged for the twelfth, there was only one thought in my head. *Winning in style.*

'It's time for the stopper,' I thought. 'The showcaser. And I'm knocking him out.'

It's funny how life turns out sometimes. With 2 minutes and 23 seconds left on the clock, the exact opposite happened as Wilder decked me with a powerful combination: a left jab, a right hand to the side of the head and then a left hook across my chin. For a moment every ambitious thought I'd had in my head went sideways because I was briefly unconscious. My brain wobbled as the ref counted down my title hopes.

One! So I'm out on the canvas, flat on my back.

Two! My thinking is all over the place: 'What the hell has gone on here? I was on my feet a second ago, now I'm on the deck, but I haven't felt a thing . . .'

Three! Wilder's walking over to the neutral corner. He's blowing a kiss at his wife.

Four! The ref's on one knee. He's in my face. Are my senses coming together?

Five! I roll on to my knees . . .

Six! It's time to move. Though I've been out for a few

32

seconds, everything feels clear. I know exactly what I'm going to do. *I'm hitting Wilder into next week.*

Seven! 'OK, no problem, you sausage,' I think. 'I'm going to give it to you . . .'

Eight! Finally I'm upright. There's 2 minutes left on the clock, give or take. My lights are back on.

Nine! The ref's shouting now. He's asking me if I can carry on. I put my arms on his shoulders and nod my head up and down. I'm staring into his eyes. *Yes. I'm OK.*

Game on.

I'd risen like the mythical phoenix from those ashes. The ref had seen it, he was stepping aside; Wilder had seen it too, though he couldn't believe his eyes, and while he was able to briefly pin me to the corner, hitting me with everything he had, I knew I had it in me to hold firm. It was time to attack because the world title was there for the taking. I put my hands behind my back at one point. Then I threw a big sweeping left hook and caught him with one or two combinations. *Bang! Bang!* When the final bell rang shortly afterwards I was convinced the win was mine, despite my two knockdowns. *Surely I'd been the better fighter overall?* But the judges had other ideas and called a draw.

I couldn't get my head around it. Nor could anyone in the arena. For a few moments it seemed as if a riot was going to kick off and I did my best to simmer the tension – by fighting on American soil I liked to think that I was acting in an ambassadorial role for England. Also, I felt fairly satisfied; there was no reason to play up because my plan had been to show the world that it was possible for a person to turn their life around, no matter how deep they'd fallen. I'd managed exactly that and in doing so, I'd landed a heavy blow for everyone struggling with a mental health problem. By not losing, I'd emerged victorious.

The realisation was as good as any title or belt.

• • •

Thousands of letters arrived at the Fury house, each one thanking me for speaking openly about my mental health struggles, before and after the Wilder bout. By the looks of it, the style in which my fight had played out was speaking volumes. I was knocked down in the final round, at a time when most fighters would have struggled to rally. But instead I shocked everyone by rising to my feet and battling on, even with Wilder smelling blood. Talk about symbolic. It was pretty much the story of my darkest years in a nutshell.

Meanwhile, the drama surrounding the tied result had elevated my status in America, big time. Suddenly, The Gypsy King was a serious deal, much larger than I'd ever been before, which felt like an important step up. Anyone looking to advance their career to the next level was required to crack the States at some point, whether they worked in sport, film or music. I used to hear it all the time. *You've got to take the USA, pal.* But top-billing status had always felt out of reach somehow, even when I'd battered Klitschko. Now the tide was turning. The manner in which I'd attacked Wilder in LA, plus that debatable points decision, meant that everybody wanted to see The Gypsy King in action on the biggest stage again – me more than anyone.

As a result I signed a lucrative TV deal with the sports channel, ESPN and another with the promoter, Top Rank, though this would make the *Fury v Wilder II* showdown a little harder to schedule, as it required what was called a co-promotion. History has shown that these kinds of deals happened rarely because the promoters involved had big egos and the negotiations could turn into a dick-swinging contest. Still, my rematch with Wilder was obviously the clash that everybody wanted to see, a contest for all the marbles. All I could do to ensure that it happened was to win my next two scheduled fights in Vegas against Tom Schwarz from Germany and Otto Wallin of Sweden. If everything went well, I'd get my second shot at Wilder.

Given that the Schwarz fight would be my debut performance on ESPN, it was important to make a splashy entrance, especially as everyone was tuning in to see the loud-mouthed Brit with a colourful backstory. *But how?*

In the end, I returned to some of the costumes I'd drawn as a kid, when I used to fantasise about my future boxing career, and landed at the stars and stripes outfit worn by Apollo Creed – the bad guy-turned-good guy from the *Rocky* films. The idea was a banger. I knew the Vegas crowd would lap it up, though I initially bamboozled everybody by walking through the arena corridors in a drab, black robe. With my movements being played on the big screens, this was nothing more than a classic sleight of hand, and once I'd started my ring walk, the robe was pulled away to reveal a pair of star-spangled shorts and a matching silk gown. Someone then plonked a red, white and blue top hat onto my head. *Glitz and glamour, baby.* The mood was completed when James Brown's 'Living in America' ripped through the PA. I strutted towards the ring, knowing I'd stolen the show.

Schwarz was twenty-five years old at the time and an up-and-coming talent, but he was fighting me too soon, even though he'd been ranked at #9 in the world by the IBF. To prove it, I spent the first round pumping him with jabs. During the second I bloodied Schwarz's nose before retreating onto the ropes and dropping my hands for fun. Then I allowed him to rip away at me with a series of free shots. For a brief moment, time seemed to come to a standstill. It was like I'd transformed into Neo – Keanu Reeves' character from *The Matrix*. I bent the fabric of reality, twisting this way and that, dodging every shot by arching my neck and jerking my shoulders. Nothing Schwarz could throw at me was going to connect and as the crowds lost their minds, I decided to turn the screw, punishing him in double quick time. *Pow! Pow! Pow!* With an impressive technical knockout, The Gypsy King had given the TV producers everything they could have dreamt of: speed, power, *cojones*.

If the demolition of Schwarz had upped my reputation, then the next fight against Otto Wallin would underline my status a fighter big on entertainment value. The Swede was another hot prospect, a 20–0 fighter ranked at #4 by the WBA, but like Schwarz, he wasn't anything for me to worry about. Or at least he shouldn't have been, but when Wallin caught me with a lucky left hook in the third, the stitching in his glove carved across my flesh, splitting open the right eyebrow and causing blood to pour down my face. A clash of heads in the fifth then opened up the skin above my right eyelid in a nasty cut that would later require forty-seven stitches. To everyone watching, I was a blood-splattered mess. My eyesight was blurred; everything was covered in red. Worse, when I walked into my corner for treatment, it turned out that my cut man, Jorge Capetillo hadn't brought the right tools with him. By the looks of things he'd been asking people around the ring for spare bits of kit. Somehow, he was able to glue my eyebrow and eyelid and by the sixth round, the doctor had given me the all-clear to continue.

I remember Ben Davison stooping down to look at me between rounds. 'How are you doing?' he said, checking over my wounds.

'*How am I doing?*' I laughed. 'My right eye's hanging out and there's blood everywhere . . . I live for this shit.'

It was true too. I knew that if I could come through and defeat Wallin, my next opponent was going to be Wilder. With an incentive like that, no one was going to stop me. Not the bloke in the other corner. Not the doctor. Not the ref. I was as fit as a fiddle and to prove it I went to war with Wallin for another six rounds, pummelling him with a series of body shots and bouncing him about with my big right. In the end I won on a unanimous decision.

Everything seemed to be moving in the right direction. Wilder won his two fights against the top ten contenders, Dominic Breazeale and Luis Ortiz, knocking them both out. By the looks of it, both of us were ready. The promoters were on board too, and a few months later, after plenty of contractual wrangling, our next big showdown, *Fury v Wilder II* was confirmed. A date had been set for 22 February 2020 at the MGM Grand Garden Arena in Vegas.

It was on.

CHAPTER THREE

LET'S FIGHT

Sometimes a person has to stand up and scrap for the thing they believe in, regardless of the noise going on around them. In the case of *Fury v Wilder II*, it was my moment to attack, literally, because after the first contest I knew a victory was in my power. Of course, everyone else in the world seemed to doubt me – *again*. They told me it was suicidal – *again*. I heard the bollocks comments – *again*. People said: 'If The Gypsy King stands and fights, he's getting dropped.' But all of that rubbish only encouraged me to grip my guns even tighter.

'I'm not going to box Wilder,' I reassured everyone. 'I'm just going to knock him out.'

What everybody seemed to forget was that last time around, I'd been in the process of shifting a load of weight, transforming myself from a fat mess into a world-class warrior. Since then, I'd grown in strength. But despite the ongoing metamorphosis, I couldn't be totally gung-ho in my approach. Wilder was a top-of-the-range knockout artist; smacking people to the canvas was what he did best. While I'd put in the performance of a lifetime against him during our first meeting, he'd very nearly punched me out in round twelve, and in doing so, I relearned a valuable lesson: when you're warring against someone that dangerous, your lights could be turned off at any second.

To increase my chances of getting a win, I invited a new trainer to The Gypsy King camp. SugarHill Steward was a bloke I'd first met in 2010, when he'd been working out of Kronk Gym in Detroit, which was owned by his late uncle, Emanuel 'Manny' Steward – the man most famous for training Lennox Lewis, Thomas Hearns and my old nemesis, Wladimir Klitschko. (Manny would later invite me to join him at the Klitschko training camp in Austria that same year.) I knew hammering Wilder would require me to build a serious knockout punch and SugarHill was the man to create it, though there would be a little turbulence as we went along. Originally, I'd wanted him to work in tandem with Ben Davison, but Ben had other ideas – he wanted to be the main man and in the end he walked away. It was a shame, Ben had known how to get the best out of me, but I respected his decision.

I loved having SugarHill around though. When he first arrived, the pair of us agreed that I should go back to basics. This might have seemed an awkward choice for a new partnership, especially seeing as I was an undefeated, lineal heavyweight champion and no one was going to teach me how to fight. *Surely I'd seen and done it all?* But, given my determination to smash Wilder, I was up for returning to some 'grassroots boxing', so that's what we did: over a period of six or seven weeks we worked on my straight punch – the big right. Meanwhile, I was encouraged to focus on the way in which I connected my quick footwork to the hands. By relearning some old tricks I received a serious upgrade.

George Foreman once said that it could be very easy for an experienced fighter to get carried away in the heat of the moment. In my case, I'd focused too much on the idea of darting out of the way of my opponent's punches. The downside to that was that I rarely looked to knock someone out during a fight. (Though I'd still picked up fifteen KOs, or technical KOs by that stage in my career.) Instead, when facing up to someone, I'd think, 'Right, I'm going to hit him and then get out of the way quick.' That had helped me to become the most elusive heavyweight in the game, *the master of not getting caught*, but it had also stopped me from doing the maximum amount of damage to the bloke in front of me. I wasn't always following up a good punch with a devastating one.

As our work progressed, SugarHill asked me to concentrate on the way in which I landed my biggest hits, over and over. The idea was to unbalance Wilder by making him sweat about what *I* was going to do, and to sharpen the technique we worked on my style for firing out powerful, single shots, two or three reps at a time. Everything was stripped back;

repetition was key, though we were very much up against it deadline-wise. SugarHill and I had started working together with around six weeks to go until fight night. It wasn't the longest amount of time to get everything locked down, but I reckoned it would be enough to do the job. We worked day after day. Hit after hit. Before long, my fists had turned into fast-moving missiles.

• • •

How I came to meet SugarHill and his uncle was a whole story in itself. As a fan of boxing, I knew all about Manny Steward and what he'd done in the sport, so connecting with him was good times. We first worked together in 2010 when I received word that Manny wanted to train me. He told us, 'If Tyson comes to Detroit, I'll make him a world champion in three years . . .' At the time I'd only just got started and Paris was pregnant with our first baby, Venezuela, so the idea of going to America was a non-starter. But a year later, once Venezuela was three or four months old, the thought of training with Manny began chewing away at me.

I thought, 'If I don't go to America, I'm going to regret it, and all my life I'll be thinking . . . *What if?*'

I'd always said to myself, 'I never want to be an if-a, would-a, should-a, could-a kind-of-person. I want to be a man who says, *I know I did everything I could to be the best that I could be . . .*'

So I decided to fly to the States.

Getting to Manny was a mission though. I had his number, but I couldn't get hold of him. I knew all about the famous Kronk Gym, which Manny ran, and that it was in Detroit, Michigan, but I didn't have an address. Like that was going to stop me. I went to a travel agent in Manchester, booked a ticket to America and got on a plane with the belief that I could manage the finer details of where I was going and what I was doing once I'd landed. My instincts were spot on. I hailed a taxi at the airport and asked the driver if he knew where the Kronk Gym was.

'Sure do,' he said. 'Get in.'

But once we arrived, what had once been Kronk Gym was nowhere to be seen. It had moved. I don't know whether I'd found the friendliest taxi driver in the world or if they were all made that way in Detroit, but the guy called around, got a fix on the location of the new Kronk and drove me all the way there. When I arrived, I walked in and dropped my bags as everyone stared. After a few nodded 'hellos' I wondered, 'So which one's my new trainer?' It dawned on me that I didn't really know what Manny looked like; I'd heard all about him, but I hadn't seen that many photos, so I went up to the ring and asked for his whereabouts.

The response was pretty moody. 'No clue. And who are you?'

'I'm Tyson Fury,' I said, before explaining that I was the

future world heavyweight champion — a comment that is now etched into boxing history.

The bloke raised an eyebrow and called out to SugarHill who was standing nearby. Within thirty minutes I was sitting in a restaurant around the corner from Kronk where his uncle was having dinner. Apparently my timing had been immaculate because Manny was only back for a few weeks, having been called into a training camp.

'It's meant to be,' he said.

Damn right it was. For the next few weeks I stayed in Manny's house. He treated me like a member of his family — I felt very much at home. Originally my ticket back to Manchester had been booked for a week-long stay, but that was soon extended to a fortnight, and then a third week because I was having the time of my life and learning so much. During the day I worked my arse off in Kronk, but at night Manny showed me around the Motor City scene as we visited restaurants and dive bars. At one point, we ended up in a karaoke joint, where everyone on the mic seemed to be a singer from the famous (now relocated) Detroit record label, Motown, or someone that had once dreamed of singing there. I couldn't help myself. I had to get up and let rip myself because, as you know, I didn't want to be an if-a, would-a, should-a, could-a kind-of-person.*

---

* I knew you were going to ask: 'Wonderful Tonight' by Eric Clapton. I smashed it.

'When if comes to talking and confidence, you're up there with Muhammad Ali and Prince Naseem,' said Manny afterwards. 'And when you've got confidence, anything is possible.'

Manny was in his late fifties at the time and a Jack the Lad; no doubt he was an OG and a lot of fun to be around. But he was also a person that commanded respect and a man of faith – one time we even went to a Catholic church together, which was just around the corner from his place. As a coach, he was fantastic. In fact, he was the first trainer that taught me how to fight as a big man. Up until that point, my main tactic was to get stuck in, my head down, arms swinging. But Manny encouraged me to avoid the punches coming my way rather than simply withstanding them.

'Don't do that,' he said, having watched me pile into a sparring partner. 'Stand up tall and box. *Use your jab.*'

Kronk was a great place to learn. I sparred with everybody in the gym, with partners rolling in and out of the ring. The place was packed with all weights and all sizes, and they all used to batter the crap out of one another – it was everything I expected from the place. The only downside was timing. Manny had to go work in another training camp, so I didn't have long with him in Detroit, but we would eventually reunite not long after in Austria, when he was training Klitschko. Manny's idea at the time was for me to move around with him, from country to country, so I could learn and improve, but I just couldn't do that. Paris and me had just had our second child, Prince John James. Rolling around Europe with Manny was the life for a single bloke with no commitments, so I was out.

I would see him again though. The most memorable time took place when I was about to fight Zack Page in 2010 on an undercard in Quebec, Canada. Manny showed up at the venue unannounced. He'd just rocked up on my doorstep, as I'd rocked up on his, only he was wearing a Hawaiian shirt, white trousers and a pair of Gucci loafers and he had nothing in the way of kit with him. Upon his entrance, the guy just looked around the room and said, 'Who's got the pads? Who's got the gloves? And who's got the wraps? Give 'em here . . .' And he warmed me up for what was a win on a unanimous decision in an eight-rounder.

Manny was only sixty-eight years old when he died and it was a real loss. He was a great man who played a big part in my career, and although I didn't get to spend a lot of time with him, we forged a tight bond. That's because everything about our friendship was meant to be. If I hadn't got on that plane and if Manny hadn't been in Detroit we'd have never worked together. And I wouldn't have hooked up with SugarHill, and become a big-time heavyweight champion. It is true what they say about fortune favouring the brave, and my gamble in flying to America with nothing more than a phone number and an idea had paid off. In many ways it was as if it had been written.

•   •   •

As my work with SugarHill progressed, one of the things I noticed was that the time flew by too quickly. One minute it was Sunday; the next it was Sunday again. I felt as if my whole career had gone by like that and on the eve of *Fury v Wilder II*, it was as if nothing more than a few months had passed since my first-ever ring walk in December 2008. I was only twenty years old back then, a lot more softly spoken, and with a lot more hair, but there was confidence to burn. I was fighting the Hungarian, Bela Gyongyosi in Nottingham on the *Carl Froch v Jean Pascal* undercard and I showed up in a white robe, my hood pulled over my head. As I swaggered through the crowd and swooped into the ring, I felt battle-ready. I'd arrived seemingly built for professional boxing.

That was nothing compared to the entrance I made in Las Vegas for my second fight with Wilder. This was a top-end production, with all the icing on the cake, and when planning the ring walk, I decided to match my Gypsy King status with a regal, red robe – the type worn by a British monarch for their coronation. A crown was even perched upon my head. For any watching viewers still unsure of the message I was sending out to the world, a commentator from Fox TV filled in the blanks:

He makes his way to the ring. The label, The Gypsy King, is not just a boxing nickname; it's ethnic pride. He's from a long line of Irish Travellers, a very specific group of gypsies stretching across the UK and Ireland and he has many Irish Traveller cousins here, Stateside. And the label, The Gypsy King, matters greatly among that nomadic group and within his bloodline. It is reserved for the toughest and best fighter among the Irish Travellers. His grandfather was the Gypsy King. His uncle was the Gypsy King. And in this, the biggest ring walk of all that any heavyweight can take, he will not walk once he comes into the arena.

The Gypsy King has decided upon a unique entry . . .

The bloke wasn't kidding. As if anyone watching had any doubts about my status as a showman, I was then carried to the ring on a throne, my procession backed by a fitting soundtrack – the 1961 hit single, 'Crazy' by Patsy Cline. During the build-up to the fight, I'd wanted something that summed up my mental health struggles of the past few years. In the end, I went for a song that was probably considered by most people to be a gentle ballad. But to me it was the perfect summary of my state of mind since 2015, especially given I was about to face the world's biggest puncher for the second time.

The thing is: I didn't choose the song; the song chose me. When I'd first put the idea to my team in the training camp, everyone had been unconvinced apart from George Lockhart. 'That'll be gangster,' he said. And he was right. 'Crazy' was unlike any other walk-in soundtrack in boxing history, where the go-to cuts were usually hardcore rap, or something heavy and aggressive. Nobody knew what the heck was going on.

Least of all Wilder.

When the first bell went, he dropped a few good punches to the top of my skull, but I soon had his number, snapping his neck back with a succession of jabs. During the pre-match hype, I'd warned Wilder that he was getting knocked down in two rounds, but my promised delivery ended up arriving a little late. As the third drew to a close, I caught him with an overhand right to the side of the dome. It was a beauty. The blow seemed to pull the canvas out from underneath him and Wilder fell like a puppet with its strings cut.

'There you go,' I thought. 'Have. *That*.'

For weeks, Wilder had been chatting about how I'd thrown soft punches in our first fight. Apparently they were like feather dusters. But on the night, they didn't seem so soft and fluffy, and Wilder didn't appear so ballsy. My big right hand, a bomb constructed in the gym with SugarHill, had turned his legs to jelly and cracked his left eardrum. I wasn't done, either. In the fifth, I sat him down again with a left hook to the body that almost knocked him out of his shoes. To anyone watching it must have looked as if he'd been swung round by a crane. Fair play to him though, he had the guts to keep on coming.

'OK, you want a bit more do you?' I said, cracking his face and busting his ears again. Blood rained from the side of his jaw. Whenever we clashed, a fountain of red sprayed across my shoulders and splattered my back and face. I looked like something from a horror film, only I was the apex predator and Wilder wasn't escaping me on the ropes. I jammed a series of pile drivers into his face, spinning him off balance. Then I worked his head until his eyes started rolling around like pool balls. Wilder was cooked and his corner threw in the towel. I'd won on a technical knockout.

As I raised my arms, he tried arguing with the official, but there was really no denying it: The Gypsy King had returned, victorious, and in doing so I'd proved to everyone that I still could pack someone like Wilder off for his lunch. But winning a boxing match was only one part of the Hollywood-style ending; the other involved my impossible psychological comeback. I'd emerged from the dark, dark days to beat back depression – the hardest opponent I'd ever faced and one that was far more dangerous than ten Deontay Wilders put together. Later that night, as I celebrated in a club, a brave new world seemed to spiral around me. I felt great, but more than anything I wanted to lie down for a good night's sleep.

Then I planned on getting up the next morning and getting at it again.

• • •

I was back, back, back. The undefeated heavyweight champion of the world, *the top of the pros*, with everything I'd ever wanted. Then, out of nowhere, the world turned to crap with the coronavirus outbreak in early 2020. Like everyone, I found the news unsettling, but from a career point of view I was also feeling frustrated. I was in my fighting prime, ready to take on the planet again, but I was being forced to retreat into my house with the wife and kids. (The good news was that everyone was in the same boat; I wasn't being stopped from fighting because of something *I'd* done.) I was lucky though; everyone around me came through unscathed, we stayed healthy, and I was able to spend some quality time with the family. As the garden became a party with barbecues, and bike rides and kickabouts with the children, I got to appreciate what was really important in life.

I then made it my mission to train three times a day from home, even spicing things up by getting Paris to work out with me, live on Instagram.* That was partly to

---

* For those of you that might be interested you can check out my workouts in my book *The Furious Method*.

keep my mental health in check – I wanted to stay busy; *I needed to*. With too much time to think, I'd learned that my mind could drift to some dark places, but exercise kept me occupied. I also knew that the boxing business would have to open up eventually and when it did The Gypsy King would be ready. Another Wilder rematch was on the cards.

The worrying reality, apart from the obvious – we were in a pandemic; there was tragedy and heartbreak all over the world – was that everything that could go wrong with my future plans was set to go bloody wrong over the next year or so. The first issue involved the contractual dealings that always preceded a fight of this kind. An agreed date of 18 July 2020 was pushed back until October, and then December, until 24 July 2021 was eventually fixed. Then, with six or seven weeks of training camp under my belt, somebody brought Covid into the gym and I ended up testing positive. Eventually, it was settled that I would face Wilder in the T-Mobile Arena in Vegas on 9 October 2021, twenty months after I'd last put him on his arse. The passing months felt like an age.

Time had been cruel. In all, I'd lost nearly five years of my boxing career: three to my mental health, and then another twenty months to the pandemic. In the grand scheme of things, this was a nothing burger, especially when compared to the nightmare experienced by some people during that first grim year or two of Covid. However, from a boxing perspective, my statistics now seemed a little bit scary. Twenty months was considered to be a long time between professional bouts and the average boxer might have felt potentially exposed in those circumstances, especially when facing someone as handy as Wilder. But you should have learned something by this point in the book: *I am not your average boxer*. My attitude? Screw it. *Let's fight.*

Somewhere in the middle of all this chaos, Wilder had started shooting his mouth off, dropping several excuses for how I'd come to beat him in *Fury v Wilder II*. All of them were rubbish, some of them were embarrassing, and his reasons were very hard to take seriously. But for the record I'll rattle them off, here and now:

1) A beauty. Wilder's ring walk costume, a heavy gown, crown and facemask, had been too heavy. By his account it had knackered him out for the fight.

2) The ref was against him.

3) His water had been spiked.

4) Someone said I'd hit him with a gypsy curse before our first fight.

5) My gloves had been loaded with something 'the size and shape of an egg weight'. (This comment had originally been started by someone online, but he was happy to talk up the theory.)

According to him, the only trick I hadn't pulled was to let him win.

Wilder was coming across as a sore loser and, as far as I was concerned, by complaining he had flushed his career knockouts and victories down the toilet, which was a shame. I'd always thought it was important to be a good sportsman, because that's what boxing was. *A sport*. Usually, there could only be one winner and one runner-up, and it was important the two combatants conducted themselves in an orderly fashion, whether they'd emerged victorious, or if things had gone south.

For example, say I'd lost to Wilder on the night (not that I would have) my reaction would have been to think: 'Fair play to the other guy. He had a better game plan. He was the better man in the battle.' Afterwards, I'd have told Wilder that I respected him. I'd have congratulated him on his success and acknowledged the hard work it must have taken to beat me. Then I would have echoed the same sentiment to any interviewer or journalist afterwards. I certainly wouldn't have gone around making a million excuses about spiked water and loaded gloves.

These were small-time concerns though; the aches and pains of living a career in battle. But then Wilder upped the stakes and crossed the line. Whereas the mood before our previous two fights had been friendly and sportsman-like, something seemed to have changed in the build-up to *Fury v Wilder III*. It seemed to me that the bloke wanted vengeance rather than reclamation of the world heavy-weight title, and out of nowhere he made a veiled threat to kill me.

'My mind is very violent,' he said on social media. 'We built a whole facility to commit a legal homicide and that's just what it is, my mind is very violent at this time. I can't wait. When you're contemplating and premeditating about harming a man and you see that person, what you've been thinking and feeling will come out.'

This wasn't the first time he'd sent out a brutal warning. Before fighting Dominic Breazeale in 2019, Wilder had claimed that he wanted to 'get a body' on his record.

'Boxing is the only sport where you can kill a man and get paid for it at the same time,' he said.

I really couldn't understand where he was coming from. It all felt a bit daft. Before every contest I'd always said a prayer that both boxers would come out in one piece.

Then I'd wish the other bloke good luck and do my best to get the 'W'. Wilder was saying online that he wanted to murder me.*

While Wilder's comments didn't make me feel ecstatic, they weren't anything to stress about either – there was no way he was going to intimidate me, or wind me up. Having said that, it made me wonder where he was in his life and why he wanted to murder someone in a sporting contest. I knew there was little point in turning an opponent into a hated enemy. Not when the chances of a potentially lethal incident happening were increased if one boxer was powered by anger, or some other negative emotion. People have

---

* OK, hands up: I did once tell Derek Chisora that I was going to kill him. In a heated press conference in 2011, I said, 'It will come down to one thing on the night: who's got the bigger heart. Who wants it more. I know that I want it so badly, nothing will stop me. I have a wife and two children to provide for. If it means killing you in the ring, that's what I'll do. To beat me you will have to kill me. You are an arrogant little prick. I'll smash your face in when we fight.'

For the record, I apologised for the comments as soon as I could and at no point did I actually mean that I wanted to *kill* Chisora. It was a defiant middle finger in a press conference. A throwaway dig, in much the same way that if a mate or family member annoyed you, or let you down, you might say that you wanted to kill them. I certainly wasn't threatening a person with 'legal homicide', or premeditating a situation where I wanted to damage an opponent.

died in the ring. Plenty others have had their lives wrecked through serious injury. I didn't want that happening in one of my fights because somebody had become too emotional, or was losing control.

It was also an attitude I couldn't relate to. Boxing is fun. The title bouts I'd been involved in – or any type of boxing match for that matter – didn't represent a do-or-die situation for me. Whenever I am in the ring, jabbing, dancing, or ducking punches, it feels like playtime, and I enjoy every minute of it. All my fights have been like that. I love goofing around and I never fight in a state of stress or tension. I certainly haven't gone into a bout with a panicked mentality. Instead, I float across the canvas, feeling relaxed and free. I live in the moment and never place any pressure on myself. That gives me a serious advantage over most fighters.

I try to carry this mindset into all aspects of life. Everything is done off the cuff, even holidays. There are mornings where I've woken up and ordered everyone into the car. 'Right! Pack up your stuff,' I've shouted. 'We're going to Bournemouth!' There have been other times when I've told Paris we were flying to Miami the next day. She knows how I am wired and has usually been up for it; I suppose it is exciting. On the occasions when she hasn't fancied an adventure, I've travelled solo. There were even times when I was out in Manchester and felt the urge to travel abroad for a night. I usually took the next available flight, arrived at my destination around midnight and then went out until five am. The next day I'd get a plane home at midday. I always had a cracking time.

That's why Wilder's chatting didn't bother me – there wasn't anything to take seriously. I knew that once his words were done, I only had to get in there and outbox him for a third time. Every threat was either flying over my head, or going in one ear and out the other. Besides, if I paid a blind bit of notice to what the other bloke was saying on the eve of every bout – how he was talking himself up, what he'd done, and what he was capable of – I'd never have stepped up to Wilder in the first place. He was a powerhouse when I first met him in 2018; there was every chance he'd still be a powerhouse for our fight in 2021. But no chance was he getting through me.

CHAPTER FOUR

FAMILY GUY

My daughter, Athena, was born prematurely at the beginning of August 2021 in the Royal Lancaster Infirmary, just two months before the third Deontay Wilder fight. The early arrival wasn't exactly a shock. Paris had predicted the baby would arrive ahead of time — because our kids tended to show up that way — and at first everything went well with the birth. I held her, meeting my new daughter for the first time, and everything was perfect. There had been no signs of anything being wrong during the pregnancy. Then the midwife plucked her out of my arms.

'I'm just going to dress her,' she said, and within minutes everything was kicking off.

Apparently her heart was beating too quickly, and at first I didn't think anything of it. Then everybody around us seemed to be panicking. Athena was hooked up to a machine, doctors were pushing buttons and taking readings and her heart rate had rocketed to 300 beats per minute, when it should have been closer to 120bpm, and there was nothing the nurses could do to fix the problem. They injected her with something that seemed to slow everything down, to around 140bpm, but then she spiked all the way up again.

The consequences were terrifying. If Athena's heart rate couldn't be steadied she would probably die from a cardiac arrest.

Watching the medical staff rushing around her and Paris was horrible, though I knew they were both in safe hands. After being born, I'd died and been resuscitated three times – the NHS had kept me going well enough. Still, that did little to ease the sense of total helplessness I was experiencing. I saw nurses sedating Athena; someone was putting a tube down her throat to assist her breathing; and while everybody seemed to be acting calmly amid the chaos, there is nothing a parent can do in a situation like that, other than to watch and pray. I'd been reduced to nothing. My baby's life was hanging in the balance and my name and what I did for a living wasn't going to change a thing.

In the end, it was decided that Athena should be blue-lighted to the Alder Hey Children's Hospital in Liverpool, and once there, her heart rate was stabilised. It was so hard to see her on an incubator, with several tubes and wires coming out of her body. She looked so tiny and vulnerable, and even though her situation had improved, the doctors were warning us we weren't yet out of the woods. Athena's heart rate was still all over the place, and at any given moment she might die. It wasn't as if we'd had one little scare and everything was suddenly OK.

As Paris recovered and Athena started her battle,

I bedded down in the Ronald McDonald House, an accommodation attached to the hospital. It was a place for parents to stay at while their kids were being cared for. Nothing could dissuade me: I was crashing there until Athena had stabilised and no way were we being separated. But every day my head span. Though it was the last thing on my mind, at some point, I was going to have to think about the upcoming fight with Deontay Wilder. If it was to go ahead, my preparation would have to happen at breakneck speed because SugarHill hadn't even arrived in the UK, and while we'd mapped out a loose training schedule, the time left to prepare was a lot shorter than I'd have liked. Training camps usually lasted for ten to twelve weeks. For this one, I only had until the first week of October to train in Morecambe. After that I was flying to the west coast of America, where I had five days to adjust to the jetlag.

Like most fighters, I tend not to work in the week building up to a title bout; it is a way of preserving energy, in much the same way that a marathon runner doesn't do any serious running in the seven days before a race. Not that I would be on easy street in Vegas. In those days before the fight I was expected to attend promotional commitments and press conferences, so there was all that to sort out too. Once my schedule was pieced together, I estimated I had around four weeks to get into fighting form. It wasn't long, but I could still make it.

At the Alder Hey Hospital the doctors were giving Athena life-saving treatment. The good news was that she'd been taken off the incubator and there were some signs of improvement, so whenever Paris and Athena were resting, I went to work. To tackle Wilder, I needed to make the most of every opportunity, and a day or so after the birth, I started a jog around the hospital with Dad. I wasn't in the best of shape at the time because I'd been struggling to eat well, what with being in and out of Alder Hey. I'd also not long recovered from Covid and my lungs felt like two sheets of sandpaper whenever I put in a shift.

Puffing a little, I'd probably only done around three miles when my phone started ringing. It was Paris. She was hysterical.

'The baby's died,' she screamed. 'The baby's dead. She's dead. *She's dead . . .*'

I sprinted to the ward as fast as I could, fearing the worst. My chest burned, my legs were in agony, and as I ran I tried my best to console Paris.

'It's going to be alright,' I panted down the phone. 'Let the doctors do their job. Don't worry . . .'

When I made it to her bedside, there seemed to be a hundred medics crowding around Athena. Apparently, she'd become completely unresponsive while Paris was holding her, then her heartbeat had faded away to nothing. Athena was resuscitated, but Paris was now losing it. A nurse was trying to calm her as the specialist staff went to work. I couldn't believe what was happening. Questions were racing through my mind. *Was my baby going to die? Was Paris going to be OK? If Athena survived, was she going to have this condition for the rest of her life?*

Eventually, to our enormous relief, and with the grace of God the doctors were able to steady Athena. We were told she would have to remain in hospital until she'd made a full recovery. In the end it would take three weeks before she was allowed home and for much of the time I slept at the Ronald McDonald House, or on the floor of the hospital ward, feeling exhausted, praying for her to pull through safely, knowing that some parents never got to take their babies home. It hurt me to see her in the cot, attached to a bleeping machine.

A lot of the time Paris and me would sit there, staring at our baby. Keeping the worrying news from the kids was a tough job too. All of them were excited to meet their new sister – Venezuela, Prince John James, Prince Tyson Fury II, Valencia Amber and Prince Adonis Amaziah.* We didn't

* When it came to the boys, I thought, 'Well, I'm the king, so I'll call them all Prince. It felt like a nice touch. The girls' names just came to us. We started with Venezuela and kept on going with the extravagant names because once you've got a Valencia or a Venezuela, you

want to tell them that Athena had nearly died because we didn't want to worry them. We've long believed that children should be allowed to behave like children for as long as possible. Frightening them at that stage didn't seem like the right thing to do.

After what felt like an age, Athena had recovered enough for us to leave hospital at the end of August — Paris, our miracle child and me. It felt like something special had happened, but I immediately went back to work, even though I probably could have postponed the fight. It's not as if I didn't have a good reason for requesting a delay. Sleeping rough on the floor of a hospital wasn't the best way to prepare for anything, let alone a world heavyweight title bout against a man who was talking up my murder. But there was no point mithering about it. I had to crack on. Turning up in Vegas, out of shape, or mentally unprepared, would only give Wilder the opportunity to do some serious damage. Apparently he was working like a man possessed with his new trainer.

can't call the next one Jane. It doesn't match. (No offence to anyone reading this called Jane, by the way. It's a nice name.) We also have some names from Greek mythology. So take Prince Adonis Amaziah: Prince is the son of a monarch; Adonis was a handsome Greek man (and Aphrodite's mortal lover). As for Athena: Athena is the goddess of war and wisdom.

And what was the point in looking for excuses? It wasn't his fault that my training plans had been ripped to shreds, or that I'd caught Covid in July, or that we'd come so close to losing Athena. Besides, pushing the fight back again would only add to the time between competitive bouts. Knowing that a positive mentality was everything in boxing, I decided to work with the cards I'd been dealt. *It was now or never.* And if anyone was thinking of underestimating me, well, more fool them. I thought, 'If this baby can get out of this hospital and get well again and beat death, then I can go over there and hammer some useless dosser – a man I've already fought twice before.'

I also had a new gym to work at, a space at Morecambe Football Club, which was only a couple of miles away from the house. I'd bought the place around the time of the first lockdown, installing a fitness room and boxing ring, and the investment was proving to be a massive game changer. Up until then, I'd moved from place to place, and at one point I was working out in Ricky Hatton's gym, which was a seventy-mile drive away in Manchester. There was also an amateur gym nearby, but whenever I showed up to rock 'n' roll, around fifty kids got about my feet, all of them wanting pictures and autographs. I found it difficult to do anything, let alone train.

In the end, I took to using the local leisure centre. I'd show up, work the cross trainer and pound the running machine before nattering to the old boys that were usually hanging about the place. I really couldn't have cared less about how the equipment looked, as long as it worked. I wasn't an influencer wanting to impress people – as long as I could do my workouts that was alright by me. But suddenly, with my own gym, I had no issues and no distractions.

October came around fast – *too fast* – and when I stepped on the scales I weighed 277 pounds, my heaviest fighting weight ever. I shrugged my shoulders and decided to get on with it. If I was man enough to take on the Wilder fight in the first place, then I was man enough to accept the consequences of it going wrong. I'd had a tough time for sure, but not as tough a time as Athena – and she'd shown the strength and willpower to fight her way back to life. I would turn her battle into fuel. I would use that experience as armour. When my moment came against Wilder, I'd know exactly what to do with it.

• • •

Recently I went on a meet-and-greet tour where I found myself answering all sorts of questions about my life – past, present and future. *Who's been your toughest opponent? What was your greatest fight? What are you going to do in your retirement?* At one event, a little boy came over. He looked up at me and said, 'What's your biggest fear . . . What are you afraid of?'

I crouched down to talk at his level. 'That's a very advanced question for a kid,' I said. 'How old are you?'

'Eleven,' said the boy.

Eleven. Wow. The lad had stumped me. After thinking about it for a little while I addressed the room and said, 'The answer to that little boy's question is: I ain't afraid of nothing. But if there's one thing that worries me, it's failing as a parent.'

It is true. Raising a family is a massive responsibility, and much bigger than I'd ever imagined it could be. Athena's illness had been a reminder of that, but there have been plenty of others, and aside from the usual stresses and scares that come from caring for a family, Paris and I have experienced a number of miscarriages. They were incredibly painful. I've also learned that the world appears to be a more dangerous place when there are kids to care for. Watch the news if you don't believe me: story after story about murderers, thieves, perverts and abusers. It has made me so much more protective.

From the start I knew it was important to be focused and present when bringing up my kids the right way because life has taught me that a person without a target is unlikely to achieve much. They are like a cruise ship without a final destination. They travel all over the shop except to the one place they are supposed to arrive at. On the other hand, a captain with an intended harbour nearly always docks at the right point, no matter how far they have to travel, or how dangerous the seas. Raising the Fury kids the right way is my destination point, as is finishing my career undefeated.

But that's because I've always been excited about having a family of my own. When I met Paris, one of the first things I asked her was how many kids she wanted. She was fifteen at the time; I was just sixteen and an amateur boxer on the up-and-up, but Paris looked at me and came up with an impressive number. *Ten*. Nearly a whole football team.

'You'll do for me,' I thought. 'Let's go.'

I'm not sure we'd be together now had she told me that raising a family wasn't in her plans, because it's what I've always wanted in life, along with being a boxing champion. But let me tell you, the success would feel pointless if I didn't have Paris and my six children, and growing older will be so much more fulfilling as a result of being with them. When a rich person hits their sixties or seventies, it's irrelevant how many Bentleys they have in their garage, or how many hot people they banged in their twenties and thirties, not if they're sitting at home, alone. Life can be rough as you grow older. If a person has placed the pursuit of money and career before family and love, they'll be in for a shock as the years roll by.

I understood that from the beginning because becoming a husband and a father changed my life. Before Paris and our first kid, Venezuela, everything was about my boxing career. Having got married, my focus then shifted to providing for the two of us. But as soon as Venezuela arrived everything changed again. I was twenty-one years old and making my way up the pro ranks, but providing for her was my main drive. Rather than thinking about what was the best move for me, or my career, I looked to what was best for the baby. Nothing else mattered. I would have happily gone without food, or walked without shoes to be the best parent I could possibly be. That love has been the same for all our kids. It hasn't dimmed one bit.

I love hanging out with them. Sometimes, such as during the school holidays, I feel like I've been taken hostage, but for the most part, it's a great laugh – I've even had a special bed made up so the whole family can squeeze in together to watch movies. Some of them are getting a little bit bigger now and I'm becoming an encouraging parent. I want them to play sports. Prince John James is trying out basketball, but he's massive for his age and he's going to be pretty heavy by the looks of it – I have no idea how good he's going to be at shooting hoops. Then again, Shaquille O'Neal was 300 pounds, so there's a chance.

Weirdly (or maybe not) the one sport I'd be really happy for all the kids to take up would be boxing. I only say *weirdly* because a lot of parents worry about the physical impact of being a serious fighter, but I've learned that boxing teaches discipline and respect, which are good values to instil in a child from an early age. If you haven't been to a boxing gym you should pop into one for a look sometime because you'll find that most kids are polite and mindful of their manners. It's because they understand what it feels to take a hit to the face. Overall though, I'll encourage all of my kids to follow their dreams, because that has been my life. The biggest regret most people have on their deathbed isn't the things they did, but the things that they didn't do.

In fact, this subject is the only thing that Wladimir Klitschko and myself have ever agreed on. *Sort of.*

He said, 'Failure is not an option.'

I say, 'Losing isn't failure; failure is not having the guts to go for something in the first place.'

A child is like a sponge: they only know what they're shown. That means they'll be interested in the path you take them on. If you're a Manchester United fan, there's a chance your kid will follow. The same applies if you're into music, art, films or martial arts. So far, I've encouraged all my boys to box – Prince Tyson, Prince John James and Adonis all love it. My four-year-old daughter, Valencia likes the training and punching too. The only one who isn't keen is Venezuela and that's because she's a lot older and is more interested in make-up and going out with her friends. How I'll feel later on in life if one of the kids turns pro and faces up to a giant in the ring, I don't know. As I've said, my mum couldn't watch me fight when I turned professional. My dad has also found it stressful at times and he's been a boxer. I suppose, as a parent, it's not the greatest, seeing your child getting lumped while everyone sitting nearby yells and screams for blood.

Even though I'm biased when it comes to boxing, being a pushy dad really isn't my thing. I'm not going to force anyone into doing something they don't want to do, because when the going gets tough, a kid will just pull out of whatever it is they're doing — especially if it hurts, like boxing. My tactics are to mind my own business, while encouraging every one of them to find an activity they're passionate about, and to surround themselves with good people. Rather than forcing something upon anyone, I'll try to inspire all the kids through *doing*, by running and training every day and grafting my arse off. If they can learn from my work ethic — where I'm up early in the morning, seizing the day, and maintaining that same energy through to bedtime — they'll be OK.

The one thing I will be pushing when it comes to my kids is the truth about how to value the real things in life. There's so much nonsense out there about the importance of being famous, or becoming a multimillionaire — especially on social media platforms — that it's all gone a bit mad. But the one thing I've learned in life is the importance of not taking what I've got for granted, like my family and friends, and my health. I even place a huge amount of value on the tiny things, like being able to wake up in a house with running water and gulping in some fresh air on my morning run; or having the freedom to buy food from the local supermarket. I nearly had all those things ripped away from me during my breakdown. Truly, it's only once everything in life has looked like it's going to fall apart, or you lose something incredibly important, like a family member, that you'll really appreciate its true value. Once it's gone, it's gone. And like a shattered mirror you can't glue it back together and expect it to look the same.

When it comes to teaching my kids what's what, I want them to have good people in their corner like I do whenever I step into the ring. I've been lucky to have the likes of SugarHill, Ricky Hatton and my uncles alongside me as I've progressed as a fighter. But the reality is that, if you're working with six losers, you're about to be one. The same applies to kids when they study at school. My children will also have to learn how to stand on their own two feet because there's nothing worse than a person who can't earn their way. That's the upbringing I came from. That's the upbringing I'll be giving to my family, because becoming independent is a wonderful thing in life.

• • •

Paris and myself come from a Gypsy background, where there are traditions and long-held values. These customs have made it difficult when balancing the type of family life we'd grown used to as kids with the challenges of modern society. For example, Catholicism is our religion and faith is very important to me. There's also no sex before marriage. But living in the Western world has made that a hard fight to win. At the same time, people in the Traveller community work very hard to keep their relationships together and divorce rates are low as a result. My advice to our children will be to make sure they're married, or at the very least in a stable relationship with someone, before having a family.

While I was growing up, I noticed that the people around me were generally wedding at a young age and starting their families shortly afterwards. Because couples often met within their local communities, there was a very good chance they'd have learned a lot about one another before even getting together, which lengthened the odds of them having a nasty surprise or two later down the line. By the time they were thirty, a couple might have been married for as long as ten years.

My mates outside of the Traveller community experience something very different. Having not settled young, they'll meet someone new and for the first five minutes they're excited. *They're the one!* When I'll then check in with them a few weeks later, it's over. *They're a crazy person!* But that's because we're talking about two people in their thirties, with their own lives and their own ways of getting on. Having gone through the first few months, they might have realised there was very little in the way of shared, common ground and they've broken up. (I'm not saying this is always the case, just sometimes.) But in Gypsy courtships, we tend to have the same interests, traditions and beliefs; we grow up together and get married young, and nine times out of ten we'll stay strong. This way has worked for generations. If it ain't broke, I see no reason to fix it.

In many ways, traditions like these made me a man before my time, but everything was geared towards growing up fast in our community. While most kids my age were in school, messing around with their mates, I was already working, earning a living and paying my way. Later, when those same kids were having a great time at college or university, or travelling around Europe, I had responsibilities. I was twenty-one when my first daughter was born and all of a sudden I had bills to pay and mouths to feed. It definitely felt like a steep learning curve, but I was up to it.

Paris came into my life when I was on the rise in boxing, representing both England and Great Britain at an amateur level – I think I'd had around two or three fights at the time. Since then we've grown up together, from kids to adults, through thick and thin, and it has ended up being a fairy story. It's also been tough in places. I'm sure it wasn't easy for Paris, being married to a twenty-something Jack the Lad; one who thought he was good-looking and was fast turning into a boxing champion.

That attention would have been tricky for her from day one because once we'd got married, I turned pro almost immediately. I was boxing on the telly. I was in the papers. Magazines and radio shows wanted to interview me all the time. So in a way, Paris has been married to someone in the public eye all her life, though if she hadn't wanted that lifestyle, she could have chosen someone else; someone more normal because I was anything but. *Abnormal* is more my thing.

It helps that Paris isn't that interested in fame. She never has been and she never will, because like me, she hasn't changed since the day we first met. She's still the same OG. Of course, loads of people have offered her a job on TV – either in a full-time role or through an occasional appearance – but she hasn't been that interested in a lot of them, mainly because we've got a family that she wants to spend time with, and Paris is happy with what she does. She's strong too, which is great for me because behind every good man is a better, more robust woman. There's no doubt she's propped me up from time to time, especially when my mental health collapsed. Her support and understanding has been everything.

That's been most obvious whenever I've had to ready

myself for a fight. Around ten to twelve weeks beforehand I'll lock myself away from the family in a training camp, which is a lonely place for me to be in because I'm a people person. I don't like being on my own; I need interaction all the time. In fact, the only time I'm by myself is when I go to bed in those months before a fight. I don't do meditation, I don't need an hour a day of my own space, and when I'm on a long car journey I'll immediately call someone up for company. Working away from the Furys is no fun for me, but it's important to have zero distractions and a family as big as mine brings plenty of them.

Paris has always understood that these periods of separation have to take place and she is OK with the time apart. Really, it has always been that way for us, we don't know any different and that same rule applied even when training for the third Deontay Wilder fight, after Athena's troubled birth. Once our new daughter was in the clear and Paris had recovered, I only had a month to get ready, and though the camp was based at my own gym in Morecambe I still stayed away from home for the most part. (I went home at weekends to see everyone.) As hard as it was to be away from my family in the circumstances, training had to be my new priority; I had to block out whatever was going on in The Outside World.

That's because when it came to fighting Wilder I needed to think strong to stay safe. The bloke was a big hitter and

I hadn't prepared as much as I would have liked. Not that it was stressing me out. As far as I was concerned, I was winning; the other bloke wasn't, and my mind was prepared enough. It's just that I wasn't there for the good of anyone else. I was doing a job, before heading home to the family, fit and healthy. *My happy place.*

CHAPTER FIVE

END GAME

I rarely watch my old fights back. In the aftermath of a title bout, during those mad hours when everyone is celebrating in the ring and I am normally serenading Paris or the fans with a song or two, the buzz can be big. I'm on too much of a high. Once I get back home, or to the hotel, I might look at the highlights on TV or scroll to a few videos on social media, but only for a few minutes. I'm really not one for living in the past. The fight is done. *Gone.* I'm more about living in the now.

Watching old bouts also gives me anxiety, even though I know the outcome. *I'll be the bloke lifting his arms in victory at the end.* But I still feel weird about it, and I'm not sure why. (Isn't that one of the biggest problems with mental health issues? If everybody knew exactly what was creating the problem in the first place, the healing process would be a lot easier.) It could be the emotional stress involved in replaying a time when I've been battered about the body and head. Or maybe it drops me back into the ring psychologically. I can feel myself taking the big hits again, and as I watch the images on screen I often physically slip the punches and move my body.

It's a shame I can't study my old matches more often because the third Wilder meeting was an absolute epic. And it all began with the build-up. Until meeting me, Wilder hadn't experienced defeat, and while he wasn't intimidated during our first two contests, he must have been mentally destroyed by the results, particularly the manner of my emphatic victory in the second fight. In the aftermath of that, he was forced to accept a difficult reality for the very first time. Previously, the thought of getting absolutely battered by an opponent must have seemed like an impossibility. A fiction. Then, faced with a nightmare come true, there was only one of two options for him to take: 1) Accept the beating. Or, 2) Magic up an alternative, bollocks reality, one in which he'd somehow emerged a champion (because, in his head, he hadn't lost fairly). Wilder ended up going for option 2. But I wasn't going to let him wind me up in any way because when it came to the type of mind games needed to dominate the headlines before a fight, I was a master, like Professor X – the *X-Men* mutant with telepathic powers so intense that he could affect another person's thoughts from 250 miles away.

During interviews I have always made a point of wriggling inside the head of an experienced opponent, usually with just a few choice words, and I have psyched-out reigning champs like Klitschko at weigh-ins and media events. Meanwhile, anyone hoping to have a go at me in the build-up to a title bout is plonked onto an emotional roller coaster. The ride shakes them up, corkscrews them around and chucks them into a loop-the-loop. Having been spat out at the other end, feeling totally wrecked, most of my rivals are left thinking, 'What's what?' And 'Who's who?' From that moment on, they see a different person every time they look at me. And it always freaks them out.

I also get to know about a person's heart in these moments. I learn who is up for it and who isn't; I discover which fighters are ready to win and which ones are ready for a paycheque. When the time came for me to face Wilder in the ring for the third time, I knew he was there for the taking again because he'd sat through our LA press conference in June, wearing a pair of sunglasses and a set of headphones. That had revealed a serious lack of self-belief. Really, what could I have possibly said to a man that was going to make him perform so badly that he had to drown me out with music?

There were no such fears from me. I had rocked up in a white suit with a print design featuring my own face, plus a white baseball cap that I'd turned backwards. (I was top-less underneath.) Wilder proceeded to say nothing for the entire event, other than to thank Jesus and his lawyer, and to utter another threat: 'Look, enough said. Time to cut off his head. And come July 24, there will be bloodshed.' When he later stepped up for the face-off and pulled away his shades, he glared. So I glared back, and we locked eyes for nearly six minutes in what was probably the longest stare down in boxing history.

Neither of us said a word: Wilder because he was hanging on to his vendetta; me because I didn't have to go there – I knew the 2020 victory had come about because I'd been the better fighter. But there was undoubtedly a war of wills going on. Whoever turned away first in that moment would have looked the weaker man and for a while, the whole room fell silent, apart from the clicking of cameras. Then slowly the shouting had started. I heard people calling out insults. Someone even tried to end the conference, but I was never going to look away. In the end, Wilder had blinked first. He put on his shades and walked. If he'd wanted to, I'd have happily stood there for days, just staring, staring, *staring* . . .

'Thank you for turning up to this one-sided press conference,' I said at the end.

I think my desire to win in anything, even a face-off, comes from my faith. It reminds me of the attitude shown by the biblical figure, David – a boy who possessed the minerals to take on the giant Goliath with nothing more than a sling and five stones plucked from a nearby stream. David was fearless and I am the same. As well as being undefeatable in the ring, I have no way of knowing when I am beaten; I never feel as if I've bitten off more than I can chew, and I never say die. Wilder was discovering all of this for himself, the hard way.

• • • •

Every punch during *Fury v Wilder III* seemed to happen in shadows and camera flashes. Due to the hits I took in the fight it's very difficult for me to piece it together, but what I can remember is that from the start I felt strong but loose as I moved around the ring. Then Wilder came at me with a series of stooping haymakers to the body – straight right-handers that connected downstairs – but I knew to keep my eyes out for a heavier shot. I'd read the script. This was a diversionary tactic.

'He's going over the top in a minute with a big one,' I thought.

Having figured out his game plan, there was really no point in me blocking the body shots because when his right-hander to the head eventually arrived, I knew that ducking it would take some focus.

I thought, 'I can't let him back me up like this.'

I caught his first few attempts early enough, glancing most of them away. Then I hit him back, bloody hard, with a searching left and a hefty right.

Being aggressive with a fighter like Deontay Wilder is the only way to operate, because he has a killer instinct, in the same way that Wladimir Klitschko had a killer instinct. In order to win I needed to hurt him and then carry on hurting him, because there was a good chance he could knock me out if I didn't. I threw a couple of big punches in the second, wobbling his head. Then I knocked him down in the third, first bouncing him off the ropes with a powerful jab and then slamming him with a heavy right. As he toppled to the deck like a tree snapped in half, I caught him twice more, believing the fight was already done.

'You're getting an early night tonight . . .' I thought.

But Wilder wasn't yet ready to go and after a check from the ref, he was deemed fit enough to fight on. I'd been complacent, and once the bell rang out on the third, and the fourth got underway, he put me to the floor – not once but twice. The first coming from a heavy right-hander that swept me over. The second: another big punch to the top of my skull. I tumbled just as the bell was about to go, but pulled myself together to make it through the round. It was a reminder to never underestimate my opponent again.

SugarHill sat me down in the corner. 'Get back on your jab,' he yelled. 'Use the jab. *Use the jab . . .*'

Most people watching probably thought I was finished. *Nobody gets knocked down twice in a round and goes on to win.* But I knew the fight was still up for grabs. Don't forget: I was like David, the kid that didn't back down from a fight.

[LEFT]
A showdown for the history books.
94,000 punters at Wembley
Stadium – the biggest ever crowd
for a European boxing match.

[LEFT AND BOTTOM]
The Gypsy King and his throne.
In case anyone watching had
any doubts about my status as
a showman.

[TOP] I was disappointed in Whyte's no-show at the press conference, but I let him have it anyway . . .
[BOTTOM LEFT AND RIGHT] . . . and at six foot nine I towered over him at the weigh-in.

All I needed for Whyte was one opportunity; an opening in which I could land a knockout punch and finish the fight.

I slung out a series of jabs and searching hooks and there was nothing he could do to evade them. Whyte had become a pain magnet. Everything I threw was landing.

Whyte collapsed backwards like a demolished tower block folding in on itself and even though he hadn't been knocked unconscious, the ref had seen enough.

A crowd mobbed me. Title belts were wrapped around my shoulders. I saw SugarHill, I saw Paris, my dad. But first I had to tell Whyte, 'You didn't fight a world champion tonight. You fought a legend in the game. A legend who can't be beat.'

At the press conference for *Fury v Wilder III*.

Between my mental health and the pandemic, I lost nearly five years of my boxing career. When someone brought Covid into the gym in June 2021, I ended up testing positive and our fight was delayed again until October.

I love making a grand entrance. I'll say to my team, 'Right, I'm coming out dressed as a Spartan,' and the magic happens from there.

After *Fury v Wilder II*, Wilder dropped several excuses for how I'd come to beat him. Apparently, his heavy gown and mask had knackered him out for the fight. He came out in this for *Fury v Wilder III* and I still beat him.

Every punch during *Fury v Wilder III* seemed to happen in shadows and camera flashes. Due to the hits I took in the fight it's bloody hard for me to piece it together, but what I can remember is that from the start I felt strong but loose as I moved around the ring.

I kept working away, picking my moments for the biggest punches, inflicting damage whenever I could.

There was no getting up from this; Wilder was asleep
before he'd hit the floor. Our epic battle was over.

I looked across the ring at Wilder. 'Right, you've been down in round three,' I thought. 'I've been down twice in round four. We'll now see who's got the most mental toughness.'

Then I remembered back to our staring contest in LA. If that showdown was anything to go by, I was the one coming out on top.

The following five rounds turned into a war of attrition — a place where I always come alive. There was no way on earth I was putting down my guns, even though the effort required to stay in the battle was exhausting. I kept working away, picking my moments for the biggest punches, inflicting damage whenever I could. At times, Wilder's legs went wobbly; he was tiring and for a while he seemed to be barely hanging on. I got behind my jab, just as SugarHill suggested, and from time to time I gave out some chat, usually in the seconds after I'd clobbered him around the skull.

Bang!

I smiled.

Did you like that you big dosser?

Then I bit down on my gumshield and went again.

Here's the general order of events when people give up during tough times: firstly, the head decides it's done; then the body follows. I've learned through experience that the trick is to not let the mind fail in the first place, and during situations like the one I found myself in against Wilder, I am able to keep any negative thoughts at bay with a series of psychological techniques. The first is to remember my previous career victories because they tell me I have it in me to win – and luckily there are a lot of them to choose from. Once the challenge has started, I then engage in an internal war of words.

The first voice is always gentle. *Oh, you're tired. You can quit . . .*

Then a second, angrier voice kicks in. It winds me up and makes me mad, forcing me into a battle with my own mind. *Go on then, quit. I dare you, you little shithouse. Do it!*

That is usually enough to get me through.

The second technique focuses on an understanding of time and pain. Quitting takes a second, but living with the hurt of failure can last a lifetime, and in those rare moments where I've given up on something minor I have always felt awful afterwards.

'Shite,' I'd think. 'Why have I just quit on that?'

Remembering back to those moments of frustration always gives me a boot up the arse, while helping me to hit my targets in whatever it was I'd been doing. There have even been times in training camps when my strength and conditioning guy has told me to do a certain type of weight, or a movement, until failure. I'll always give him a look.

'Listen, you'll have to give me a goal, even if it's an outrageous one, because I ain't quitting. There will be no burnout and I'll be here until tomorrow morning.'

As far as I am concerned there is nothing worse than downing tools on something, and even the thought of it *potentially* happening annoys me. While I've never experienced defeat in my pro career, and can't even imagine it, if I do ever lose a fight to a knockout punch – a lucky shot I couldn't have protected myself against – I might be able to accept the loss. *Maybe*. But if I were to throw in the towel due to a broken jaw, a twisted ankle, or a split head, I couldn't stomach it. So I don't allow it to happen.

I've learned that there's really no stopping the mind. Some people out there (not many) can even push way beyond the limits of what's assumed to be humanly possible, simply through self-belief. I'd like to think that I work in pretty much the same way; I won't stop to find out what my limits are. For example, I could run a marathon tomorrow without training, due to the simple reason that my brain wouldn't allow me to stop moving. I could go on to one of those brutal reality TV shows, where the contestants have to survive on their mental strength, and clean up, no problem, because the mind controls everything in situations where a person has to face their breaking points. Mine would be well suited because it's as strong as concrete.

But it's not just about running around like a headless

chicken, because I believe in quality over quantity. No matter what the task or challenge is, it has to be done right. It doesn't matter whether I'm training for a heavyweight championship bout or washing the car, I'll put the same level of passion and commitment in to both. If it's training, I'll force my body and mind beyond the limit, over and over, and over.* If I'm cleaning the car, I'll soap it down two or three times before hosing it off. Then I'll take the chamois leather to it. I don't do half measures; everything's got to be performed correctly otherwise there's no point me doing it in the first place.

• • •

Deontay Wilder was about to witness my mental strength up close. I caught him again in the tenth with another big

---

* Partly, this attitude is down to my OCD, but while it helps to work hard and to never give up, there are aspects of it that are a hindrance. I'll drive myself mad over stuff I really shouldn't be getting worked up about. Like if I'm packing the shopping away at the supermarket till. The fresh meat has to go in a bag with all the other fresh meat; the cleaning stuff has to go in a bag with all the other cleaning stuff; the tinned goods need to go in the same bag too. I can't just chuck it all in together and be done with it, like most people would because it gives me really bad anxiety. This type of mindset can be bizarre at times.

right-hander that knocked him to the canvas. For a second I put my arms up, believing the fight was done. Then I snapped out of it, remembering my mistake from the third. *There's no point admiring your work against this guy. He could come out swinging again.* I took a step back and assessed the state of him.

'If you get up, pal, I'll knock you down again,' I thought. 'If you don't, then see you later.'

Wilder was wobbling, rising to his feet; there was a little fight left in him, but not much.

'Do what you've got to do,' I told myself. 'And if he's going to keep coming, then keep delivering the shots . . .'

By the time the eleventh round had kicked off, I knew my opponent was done, even though he'd managed a little row of punches towards the close of ten. He was getting weaker and weaker; I was moving very aggressively and smacking him about with hammers. I caught him with a solid right. Then another. A powerful uppercut rocked him back. I thought, 'If I can knock him down again, he won't be getting back up.' And once I'd manhandled him a little bit, pushing him away to give myself enough space for a bigger hit, I spotted my opportunity.

I caught him with a left hook and then a big right hook. I felt my knuckles sinking into the side of his head through the glove – it was like I'd pounded my fist into a block of wet clay. To Wilder, it must have felt as if all 277 pounds of me had connected with his brain and his face shook like a plate of jelly as he went over. There was no getting up from that, Wilder was asleep before he'd hit the floor, and I ran to the ropes, jumping up to face the crowd. Our epic battle was over.

And he could have no excuses this time.

At the end of the fight, I struggled to piece together the big events. That was partly down to the chaos on the canvas afterwards – the shouting and the celebrating – but something felt off. Everything was foggy; I couldn't remember exactly what had happened and for a little while I didn't know what was going on. The basics were there. *I was in Vegas; I'd beaten Wilder.* But parts of the match seemed out of reach. There were blanks, so I kept asking my brother, Shane, a load of questions.

How many times did I put him down?

How many times did he knock me over?

What round did the fight finish in?

When I reached around to the back of my skull I felt a lump forming, a war wound from one of the blows Wilder had managed to glance across my head. My heart sank. You never knew what those lumps could be, especially when you've been clumped by a bloke of Wilder's size. Those pummelling bangs to the skull, in a fight that had nearly lasted the distance, would leave a serious mark. *Was I going to suffer from brain swelling?* I'd heard horror stories of fighters having to go through surgery to sort a serious head injury, I also knew of boxers that had been left brain-injured.

After the canvas had been cleared, I went to see the doctor. 'Check me over quickly,' I said.

The doc ran a series of tests. 'Is everything OK?' I asked.

'Yeah, everything's fine. You've got some swelling on the head, but there's no proper damage. You're OK . . .'

I knew I'd been in a war, so I couldn't imagine how Wilder must have felt seeing as he'd also been punched in the head repeatedly. Before seeing the doctor I had walked over to chat. It was time to let bygones be bygones. We'd had a fantastic fight after all, but when I approached him there was nothing in his reaction that suggested a truce was coming. Wilder didn't want to talk.

'I don't respect you,' he said.

In his mind, the fight was still personal. 'That's OK. It's your loss,' I said. 'And you're a sore loser.'

With hindsight, it might not have been the best time to approach Wilder. He had just been knocked unconscious so there's a chance he might have been delirious. But also, the fact that he'd threatened to kill me in the build-up had probably altered his emotional focus. I wasn't going to pay too much attention to his words; I was continuing on my own path as always. That night we went to the high-end Hakkasan nightclub in Vegas and burned through a ton of money in an hour, buying drinks for everybody.

My head felt fixed right up after that.

CHAPTER SIX

THE U-TURN

Remember earlier when I said that everyone usually has a plan until they've been punched in the gob?

Well, here comes the hit.

As the dust settled on the Wilder fight, it felt like the time for me to hang up my gloves had finally arrived. *Again*. I was healthy and if I walked away I'd have zero regrets, knowing in my heart of hearts that I'd given everything to the sport. The good-time vibes would be cranked up even higher if I retired without a loss to become the only living member in an elite club featuring two people: Rocky Marciano and myself, the undefeated heavyweight champions of the world. To me, that was more rewarding than any belt or knockout.

And then . . .

. . . *Bang!* Frank Warren approached me with the opportunity to fight at Wembley Stadium in April 2022.

I took a breath. The pros of accepting the bout were easy to figure out. For starters, it was bound to be an epic battle on home soil. But it would also mark my first appearance in the UK for nearly four years, the last being my comeback match against Francesco Pianeta in Belfast in 2018. Since the beginning of 2020, the country had been locked down, on and off, due to the coronavirus pandemic, and after all that time, with the hardship and pain that came with it, England seemed to be peeling itself off the canvas for another go around. A sporting event at the national stadium, packed with tens of thousands of boxing fans, would only add to the idea that we were healing as a nation.

But I was pushing my luck because being able to consider retirement at the age of thirty-three was incredible, a gift, and the work required to even reach that point had been back-breaking, as it would have been for any combat athlete in my position. Yeah, most elite-level fighters are millionaires, but there is a simple truth to our lives: we graft so bloody hard for our money.

This isn't exactly news. I was warned about the hardships of becoming a pro boxer as a kid, having been selected to represent England at amateur level, and while training abroad one time, a coach had gathered all the lads around for a pep talk. The chat was revealing.

'Look, the road's going to be long,' he said. 'And you'll have to sacrifice things you never thought you'd even dream of sacrificing to get to where you want to be. Even then, 80 per cent of you won't make it.'

But I had made it. I was in a place where the sacrifices could stop – I only had to say so. And yet, here I was, considering another fight, for another purse, in another throw of the mortality dice. And all at the moment where I'd emotionally accepted my exit from boxing.

So of course I said yes.

First of all, I told Paris. 'I've got to fight again.'

'Why? You said you weren't going to do this,' she said.

'I know. *I know.* But I owe the fans one more fight—'

She pushed back. 'You told me it was over. And if you take this fight, then what? There's always going to be one more, isn't there?'

'But what about all the people who haven't been able to see me fight live in the last four years?' I said. 'All the people that stayed up until four in the morning to watch me fight in America? What about all the people that would love to see me live, one last time?'

We got into it a little bit. There was no denying that Wembley was a showcase venue, an opportunity to bow out in style.

I said, 'Paris, by going out this way, I'll be giving the UK's boxing fans what they want: The Return of the Mack. The Boys Are Back In Town. Me: going out with a massive bang. It'll be the cherry on a fantastic cake.'

How could it not be? Throughout my career, the fans have been absolutely crazy. They've travelled the world with me, standing by my side for a long, long time, even when the chips were down. I've seen them packing into the seats at the Staples Center in Los Angeles and Madison Square

Garden in New York, some of the biggest boxing venues in the world. The scenes for the *Fury v Wilder Trilogy* had been crazy too, but that's because our nation produced the best fans in the world – the loudest, the drunkest, the rowdiest. Whether it is football, rugby or boxing, were known for out-singing anyone, and my London showdown was bound to be a banging night out. Guaranteed. A day on the lash with friends, a few beers at Wembley and then a massive session afterwards to celebrate. Could it get any better for a boxing fan?

'Paris, I want them to have a massive get-together in their own back garden,' I said. 'Rather than them saying goodbye on the other side of the planet.'

In the end, she came around. 'OK, OK. You're right. You do have to fight again.'

Everything was sorted. Boxing was about to have the mother of all parties.

• • •

While the Wembley showdown presented an incredible opportunity to go out in style, there was still plenty to think about, the first thing being my opponent. The WBC president, Mauricio Sulaimán had made it known that any mandatory title defence would have to take place against Dillian Whyte, and the bloke was a worthy challenger. At

6 foot 4 and 18 stone, the then 33-year-old (he would be thirty-four at the time of the fight) with only two losses on his record (one defeat to Anthony Joshua in 2015 and another to Alexander Povetkin in 2020) had knocked out some pretty solid fighters on his way to becoming a British champion. For a time, Whyte had even made it to the number one ranked WBC contender position in the heavyweight division. Here was a dude I was going to have to take very seriously indeed.

But I take all my opponents seriously, always. I'm certainly not in the habit of underestimating a highly trained heavyweight title fighter, because everyone in my category carries the potential to come at me really hard with a knockout punch. Not that I ever visualise it before a fight. Just thinking about getting sent to the canvas invites the possibility of it actually happening, so it is an image I blank from my head, in much the same way that a weightlifter erases doubt before attempting a personal best. To step up to the bar while thinking, 'I can't lift this . . .' Well, that's only going to end in disaster, isn't it? As I've said before, the mind is the most powerful resource on the planet and capable of incredible feats, so I was rocking up to Wembley with only one thought: I'm knocking this fella out.

Interestingly, Whyte and I share a little history. After I'd won the British, Irish, WBO inter-continental and

Commonwealth heavyweight championships and he was taking names as an emerging boxer, I invited him into my training camps to spar. This was an invitation I was committed to, because as a youngster I wasn't treated so well when stepping into the worlds of one or two pro fighters. After a few bad experiences, I made it a point to look after everyone I employed, especially sparring partners, who are an integral part of my training group – like eggs in a cake, whisked in. From the minute they arrive, I want them to feel like a fully fledged member of the Fury team with total access to the five-star facilities, plus money for good food and a car to use – a nice one, not a banger. They are also given 24/7 access to chefs, massage therapists, physios, and strength and conditioning trainers. Once the work is done, every single one of those sparring partners wants to return for the next fight.

Training camps are a gruelling business and I take care not to wear anybody out. I want my sparring opponents to feel fresh, all the time, because it guarantees a better session, but my style of working is very different to that of a lot of boxers, some of whom like smashing their guys to bits. Instead, I bring three or four blokes into the camp and none of them are allowed to spar for more than three rounds at a time. Once their nine minutes are done, I'll bring the next one in, even if the first fighter has been buzzing about the ring, seemingly ready for more. By doing so, I spend my entire sessions warring with a fast, sharp guy, which makes it so much easier to pick apart a tiring opponent when the real fight comes around.

For a while, Whyte had been a part of that set-up and I'd brought him in as far back as 2012 after he'd been suspended. When he arrived he was treated like every sparring partner I'd invited into the camp: we ate the same, we drank the same and we trained the same, and I think we initially got along because at the time we both had similar goals. More than anything, Whyte had ambition to burn, just like me. After that, I took him under my wing for a bit because I liked him, he was an all-round decent fella who sometimes leant on me for fighting tips, and if ever an opponent made Whyte's life difficult early on in his career (which wasn't often), I sent a supportive note to keep him going.

Chin up, pal. This is what happens. It's part and parcel of boxing.

We ended up hanging out away from training and I remember the pair of us sparring together in 2013. The camp was in a Dutch town close to the Belgium border and every now and then we'd head into Antwerp and wander from bar to bar. Me dressed in a full-on fur coat, Whyte in a leather jacket; I looked like a pimp, he looked like a debt collector. But despite our past friendship, it would be me coming to collect at Wembley because I had his number, like I had everyone's number. And he bloody well knew it.

• • •

As with my previous fights, the Wembley showdown was being organised by my promoter, Frank Warren. A powerful figure with over forty years of experience, Frank has looked after the likes of Ricky Hatton, Amir Khan, Frank Bruno and Chris Eubank. In fact, he's been in the business for so long that the things Frank *doesn't* know about boxing probably aren't worth knowing in the first place. I chose him as my promoter while preparing to fight again in 2018, even though I must have looked like a bad bet. At the time I was still massively overweight, coming in at around 26 or 27 stone, having been away from boxing for around 1,000 days. Despite the mess I was clearly still in, Frank reckoned he could secure me a series of big fights and even bigger paydays.

'Well, if you believe in this,' I said, gesturing to my body, 'you must believe in magic.'

From then on, Frank had a new nickname, *The Magic Man*, and he promoted those comeback bouts against the Albanian, Sefer Seferi and Francesco Pianeta of Italy.

This wasn't my first experience of working with Frank. I'd initially met him in 2014, having signed a deal with his TV channel, BoxNation. From there, I fought Joey Abell and defeated Frank's fighter, Derek Chisora, during our second fight. But beyond our work together, I never had much involvement with Frank and didn't know a lot about him. I still don't. The only thing I care about is the fact that he is a boxing promoter and a big-time one at that. I couldn't tell you whether he whips up an amazing omelette, or if he has some other unknown talents, because we don't talk that way. Frank Warren is the promoter and I am the fighter; his job is to put the fights on, mine is to win them; and the only time he ever calls me up is if there is a deal to be discussed. We are simply business, baby.

Frank had set the Whyte fight for 23 April and when Wembley Stadium was officially announced as the venue, a lot of people – who should have known better – assumed it was a joke. Around 90,000 tickets were set to go on sale and at first I heard all the usual negative bollocks doing the rounds about how the seats wouldn't be sold. *Why doesn't Tyson Fury do a normal venue? We've just had a pandemic, no one will want to see this. Blah, blah, blah . . .* But when the box office opened, 85,000 tickets flew out in around three hours and Frank had to request permission so he could sell even more. In the end, we shifted 94,000, which gave *Fury v Whyte* a post-war record for a boxing match. My gut feeling had been spot on. After over a year of lockdowns the country was in desperate need of a big night out.

I can't understand why people were surprised. I've been a salesman all my life, starting from when I was a kid working in the car trade. More than anything I know how to drum up interest with the tyre kickers and the undecided. That means, when it comes to boxing, I understand what it takes to sell an event to anyone that might be sitting on the fence. I suppose in many ways I haven't actually needed a promoter during my career. Don't misread me: I'm not taking anything away from Frank Warren, but it is his job to organise the show, the logistics and the TV rights. The rest I do with press conferences and PR stunts, going all the way back to my public appearances before the Klitschko fight when I rocked up in a Batman costume. People might think that promoters have done wonders for me during my career; I'd argue that it was *me* doing wonders for *them*. I am a dream client. Given the way in which I both fight and present myself, a priest with zero understanding of boxing could have promoted *Fury v Whyte* and still sold out the place in a day or two.

● ● ●

While the fight being held at Wembley Stadium was undeniably a big deal, the venue didn't hold a special or sentimental spot in my heart, not like some places do. While mapping out my fighting career as a young kid, the national stadium hadn't been on any of the wishlists. I'm a Man United fan so I've always quite fancied appearing at Old Trafford. Apart from that I've lived out my boxing dreams, fighting in the clubs and arenas I saw on TV a kid. One of those is York Hall in Bethnal Green, east London – a proper place with a proper history, even though at the time I fought there it was a dingy and derelict dump with tiny changing rooms. Anyone who is anyone has boxed there, and I have experienced it a couple of times – once in the ABA finals as a teenager, and then when I was working my way up in the pro game. People from all over the world know about York Hall. It is considered a mecca for UK boxing.

Another venue I'd always dreamed of fighting in was Madison Square Garden, New York, me dishing out big hits under the spotlights. I made it there in 2013 having beaten Steve Cunningham during my first-ever pro appearance in the US and when I knocked him out in the seventh round my ambition soared.

'This is it now. *I can't lose*. I'll become world champion, because if you can do the business in New York, the world is your oyster . . .'

The other venue my younger self had always fantasised about fighting in was the Staples Center in LA, where I'd first taken on Wilder. It was everything I'd hoped it would be: the place was packed, everyone going crazy.

Having ticked off those dream locations earlier on in my career, I was in good shape for a fight the size of Wembley Stadium. There was no stress about the scale and expectations. I was never a person to get rattled by stage fright anyway, and at no point did the prestige of the event bother me. I wasn't one to freak out and think, 'Oh my god! I'm about to fight in front of 94,000 people. How will I cope?' As long as I trained and prepared in the right way, I was going to be more than OK and in many ways, I was a bit like a schoolkid walking into exam season knowing the revision had been nailed. (Not that I would know what that was like.)

I was also dripping in confidence at that time, which, as you should know by now, is a strength of mine. Supreme self-belief is vital to win and it's not something that can easily be manufactured. I've noticed it oozing from some sports stars, and I've seen it fading away in others. The Manchester United and Real Madrid legend, Cristiano Ronaldo is a classic example of this idea, especially when he was in his prime. If ever he stepped up to take a free kick, he looked a dead cert to succeed.

As I prepared myself for the biggest sporting event of the year, I was going to be like Ronaldo: focused and ready to work, though I wasn't going to overdo it — I didn't want to train so excessively that some last ounce of energy, or a crucial punch was left behind in in the gym. Ultimately I was there to put on a show. Even if the fight became a struggle, I'd still find a way to beat Whyte. So I stepped into my training camp, ready to go, willing to work, desperate to perform.

CHAPTER SEVEN

IT'S NOT ALL SUNSHINE AND RAINBOWS

At the beginning of December 2021, I started early with an eight-week programme in which I jogged every morning and trained every evening. I made sure to cut back on the fish and chips too. At that point, I was already in better shape than I had been during the chaotic build-up to *Fury v Wilder III* and I even worked through Christmas, which helped to keep the black dog of depression on a leash. I've noticed that my mental health issues sometimes build up during the festive season, when it feels like Groundhog Day for around a fortnight, and it becomes hard to tell Sunday from any other day. In those disorientating moments, my weights, bags and the pounding of my trainers on the pavement keep me strong.

By February, SugarHill had arrived for the training camp I was operating out of my Morecambe gym. At the same time, I moved into another house to avoid the distractions that a six-strong battalion of kids could bring. From there, my workload went into overdrive and the target was clear to everyone. *Get me to the fight injury free, then wind me up and watch me go.* I wanted to test myself to the max throughout, so we brought in a group of fearsome sparring partners, young fighters, all undefeated, each one with a point to prove. There was the up-and-coming heavyweight, David Adeleye, who had been with me during my last three camps; Martin Bakole was a 6 foot 6, 19-stone beast and had it in him to push me really hard; and, finally, Jarrell Miller was a strong guy SugarHill had invited from America.

We sparred four times a week, every week, the fighters rolling in and out of the ring over ten-round sessions. At first I felt up against it, but with time came strength and I grew into the agony. I really didn't have a problem with hurting, not when I was preparing for the fight. It didn't feel like proper suffering either because I was being helped through my sessions by a team of coaches, nutritionists and massage therapists. My body was definitely taking a battering though, especially when I was getting pounded in the stomach with a medicine ball, but as far as I was concerned, nowt that came easily was worth having. Sacrificing my personal comfort to defend a world title felt meaningful.

There was also a little pain thanks to the series of injuries I'd picked up over the years. I shrugged them off, knowing that hurt was part and parcel of being in camp. The main thing bothering me was the fallout from two operations in October 2021, when I'd gone under the knife to treat a case of tennis elbow and bone spurs. At first, the diagnosis was that

I'd developed arthritis in the elbow. Then a specialist in LA spotted some bone fragments floating around and they were later removed through surgery. The joint was then cleaned up, and my mobility returned after a series of injections had reduced the swelling, but only to around 70 per cent. I still couldn't straighten my arm fully and there were only a few months to go until the Whyte fight, but that didn't stop me from hitting personal bests on the deadlift and bench press like a Titan.

Reassuringly, my reflexes were still sharp, despite those injuries, which was good news because body movement and quick feet have always been a major part of my game. Yeah, I can hit a bloke into next week, but I am also a dancer on the canvas and I've developed the healthy habit of dodging punches, whereas some boxers rely solely on power. That is usually the last thing to go in a heavyweight boxer's armoury, which is why George Foreman was winning and retaining titles up until the age of forty-eight. He always relied on brute force rather than agility. That meant his effectiveness wasn't diminished as he aged.* I can

* I was thirty-three at the time, in the prime of my life and at the peak age range for a heavyweight. Fighters in my category are most effective in their late twenties and typically go on for another seven to ten years. Lighter fighters mature faster, but they decline faster too and are often done by their early thirties.

probably expect a different career trajectory to him, given my assets.

As I was preparing for Wilder during the camp, I reflected more on my unusual style, and my unusual body type as a boxer. One early fight in particular showcased my natural skills and glitches to the world, and that was my victory over Derek Chisora in 2011. The venue was London's Wembley Arena but the attention on me had felt so much bigger because the contest was being screened live on Channel 5. This was set to be the first live bout on terrestrial telly in ages and lots of boxing fans seemed to be making a big deal out of it. In the end an estimated audience of 2.9 million viewers tuned in to watch, though it helped that I'd done a good job of hyping up the contest beforehand. When the fight kicked off, Chisora rocked me with some big hits in rounds two and three but I steadied myself before finding my way back into the contest.

One of the commentators went crazy. 'This guy has got so many flaws, but he's so watchable and so loveable,' he shouted.

That was because I didn't look like a heavyweight boxer — I was more like a bloke from the boozer, than a ripped athlete. I went on to win the contest by a unanimous decision to take the British and Commonwealth titles.

• • •

By 2022 I had a strong support team around me in training camp. At that stage, SugarHill, with his positive energy and incredible boxing knowledge, was a part of the furniture. But in the short time we'd been working together he had transformed. When we first met before *Fury v Wilder II*, he was quiet and shy. But having hung around The Gypsy King crowd for a while, he was morphing into an absolute animal. In the gym, he sang, he danced, and he cracked jokes.

'Bollocks,' I thought. 'I've created a monster.'

I loved it when people grew in that way. SugarHill had entered my world and having seen how I lived and trained close up, he'd gathered an understanding of how I worked and the sacrifices I was making in order to succeed. With that info he was able to tap into my personality and he knew how to get me going. Luckily for him, I was a lunatic in training, raring to go, and always set to 125 per cent. It wasn't like he had to fire me up that often. It's one of the reasons why he referred to me as *The Big Dog*. I usually arrived at work, ready to battle.

The other key player in the group was my nutritionist, the former US Marine and MMA fighter, George Lockhart. George is a big man of faith and carries a serious reputation, having fed the likes of Conor McGregor. He is also one of my best friends in the world and is an unbelievable chef, who knows exactly what I need to eat and when. We started working together in 2018 and his influence was a game changer. My nutrition plan went from being wildly rubbish to a healthy (mainly) 3,000 to 4,000 calories a day as George worked to keep me on track for whatever fight was coming next. Before long, his positive influence was a habitual part of my daily life, and eating well became something I did without thinking, like putting my shoes on to leave the house. During the comeback trail, I shifted thirty pounds in thirty days. Have *that*, Davina McCall.

The other thing about George is that he has a talent for reading my moods, even when I am training hard, my head down. That is a real skill because complaining isn't my thing; I don't like telling people when I am tired or groggy. During that camp there were days when I would walk into the gym feeling terrible. But George usually noticed. Then he'd prod me with questions.

'How are you doing today?

I'd shrug. 'I'm great!'

An eyebrow would shoot up. 'Sure?'

'Yeah—'

But George knew. *He always knew.*

'I get that you feel great *all the time,* and you're going to push it no matter what. But are you tired? Sore? Leggy?'

Once I'd told him how I really was, George would whip up a burrito packed with eggs, chicken and breakfast potatoes. That usually put me right. Or maybe he'd make a poke bowl with cauliflower rice. Another thing that went down a treat was a hill of fruit, Greek yoghurt and flax seeds. So, as for the myth perpetuated by Rocky Balboa about getting up at 5am, downing a pint of raw eggs and going for a run? That couldn't have been farther away from my reality. I was eating like a king.

• • •

You might have a misconception about boxing training camps, that they're a glamorous place to be, all glitz, glamour and flashing lights. But that's bollocks. There are no rainbows or unicorns; training camps can be boring places. To most people the work would probably seem dull, painful and repetitive, though that's what I loved about it, and through March and April I ran through an identical set of drills and exercises – day after day; again and again; over and over – only breaking to eat the same lunch as yesterday, or the breakfast I'd have tomorrow. For a comparison, imagine a school where they only teach three subjects. In my case I was taking exams in exercise, sleeping and diet, all while a sparring partner smashed my body to bits.

So here's a typical day from the training camp life of Tyson Fury. I am up at 6:30am, no excuses. I wash, brush my teeth, get dressed and head downstairs. I am usually done with breakfast by around 7:00 or 7:30 and after getting my stuff together I am out the door, in the car, and walking through into the gym by nine. Following a morning of work, I break for lunch and rest up. Then I am back in the afternoon to spar. Training finished, I drive home, have my tea and try to get in bed by nine. On Mondays, Wednesdays and Fridays, I box – sometimes pad work, sometimes bag work – and I spar three or four times a week. On alternate days, I push myself through strength-and-conditioning work; maybe I go for a run. On Sundays I rest and visit the family.

Monday to Sunday. Rinse. Repeat.

Bosh.

This is a way of working I've grown accustomed to over a twenty-year life in the game. When I first started my professional career in 2008, my late Uncle Hughie trained me. Rather than moving into a fancy gym with all the mod cons, we worked out of a big shed with a barely-held-together boxing ring. The loose flooring caused me to stumble from time to time, but at least the commute was short. I was living in a caravan next door at the time, and I found comfort in an environment where the equipment was old and worn. Rough and ready was more my thing; I liked the spit and sawdust approach; and I wasn't the kind of fighter that needed to be wired up to a computer to feel prepared, or plugged in to the electric grid like a robot.

That's because there is nothing technical about smashing another dude's face in and because the basic needs of humans haven't evolved in millennia. From the beginning of time, we've done exactly the same thing as a species on the daily. We get up. We provide. We look after our families. We eat, drink and sleep. Any of the other crap that happens in between is a personal preference. The concept of fighting is pretty much the same: it hasn't evolved because it doesn't need to, and really, when you strip everything away, all you are left with is two people trying to punch each other for the entertainment of others. It was like that for the very first boxing match thousands of years ago. It's no different today.

That hasn't stopped some people from trying to over-complicate the process with all the bells and whistles. *Yoga?* That's nonsense; stretching doesn't work for me. *Ice baths?* I've had one or two, but they don't make a penny's worth of difference. The same goes for vegetables; even since George has been in my camp, I don't eat a lot of them. I am approaching my mid thirties, so if I don't want to eat my greens, I don't have to. I can also remember someone once warning me off of diet pop. I thought, 'What a load of shite,' and sank between ten and twenty a day. My attitude is that I can do what I want because it isn't holding me back from being the world champion.

Really, when it comes to training, there are three things for me to focus on. 1) Running. 2) Sparring. 3) The heavy bag. Forget the stretching, the computer analysis and all that fancy bollocks because as Andy Ruiz Jr proved when he defeated Anthony Joshua in 2019 — after coming in as fat as a pig, by the way — it's not about the sports science or the technology. If it had been, Joshua would have easily won. I experienced the same thing in my career too, when I fought Klitschko. The Ukrainian had surrounded himself with doctors, weightlifters, sports geeks and top chefs, while my training camp was running out of a tin shed in a muddy field in Liverpool and I slept in a caravan. I still lost 6 stone in the build-up to give him a hiding.

Throughout my career, a number of trainers have tried to stick heart rate monitors to my chest so I could be assessed during sparring sessions.

My response? 'Suck my balls. Because the numbers on your computer screen are going to mean sod-all when I hit the other bloke in the temple and his legs go all wobbly.'

Others have encouraged me to operate in the 'red zone', which is where an athlete uses 90–100 per cent of their maximum heart rate and everything hurts. I've hated that too. It is knackering and whenever a coach has tried to push me with numbers and percentages, I have pushed back.

'I'm killing myself here,' I'd say. 'I *am* in the red zone.'

'But you're not, the machine says you've got to keep working.'

'Screw what that machine says,' I'd shout. 'I'm fit as.'

Eight weeks later, having trained without the high-tech nonsense, I would get into the ring and blitz my opponent. Then, having left the arena victorious, I often noticed that nobody wanted to argue the toss about graphs and charts. Nobody discussed the red zone either. They only wanted to talk about the fight.

Funny that.

•   •   •

When I'm actually working, everything has to be done just right. I'm what you'd call a perfectionist. Partly this is down to the fact that I suffer from OCD, and can't stand not having everything in the right place. Though it's under control now, the issue was pretty bad for a while. Bad in that I would get pissed off if the heaters in my car weren't set to the same level. Bad that if the volume on my radio or TV wasn't set to an even number I would feel weird. Not doing those things could at times create anxiety for me. But the upside of my OCD is that if you give me a routine, I can potentially live with it for ever and I am driven to do things correctly. It makes me a very quick learner and once I'm shown something it doesn't need repeating.

That mindset is one of the reasons why I could never do SugarHill's job. Or George's for that matter. Everything has to be performed exactly the way I like it – no excuses. I also have zero patience; I don't want something done next week, next month, or even next year. It has to be today or forget about it. Throughout my career, people have always said to me: *Why are you in a rush? You want everything yesterday . . .* They have told me to wait before fighting certain people, like Deontay Wilder, but I have pressed ahead anyway. My response has usually been to tell them, 'I believe in striking while the iron's hot. I don't want to wait ten years for something to happen. I want it now.' I believe that the winning attitude needs a person to be in the moment, like so many other things.

But that isn't the right approach for a coach, and the best ones display both patience and urgency. Also, as a trainer, there is every chance I would expect my fighters to be like me. A boxer under my tutelage would have to hit like me, dodge punches like me and take pain like me. They would have to hate the thought of losing like me, and love the sensation of proving people wrong like me. Given that everyone, of course, is different, I probably wouldn't be flexible enough in my approach to be a coach.

Still, there have had to be trade-offs with my obsessive nature when it comes to performance and routine, and I have often found the best balance in the nearest pub. Yeah, the training camp environment is good for me. With a siege mentality I thrive because I know exactly when I am training, when I am eating and when I am sleeping, for three months, but I'm not going to live like a monk. I like to nip out and have a couple of pints every now and then because it helps to sort my head before a big fight. Besides, I have heard the hops are good for recovery. Don't get me wrong: I never smash it, or have a huge party. I have just learned that it is a lot harder to get the best out of me when I'm not having fun.

What makes a good boxer is a strong work–life balance. They have to play well too. If a fighter doesn't have the occasional cigar after a fight, doesn't go out for a few pints with the lads, or doesn't have a partner, they'll probably lose sight of what's important. Also, when those moments in life do come around – like when they meet The One, or encounter a period in their life when they want to blow off steam – they won't be able to handle it because it's such an alien experience. Everything feels too new. I'm not suggesting that pro boxers should go out every night and get hammered. I'm simply saying there's no harm in relaxing from time to time. Ours is a sport where if you don't enjoy life, you won't get the best out of yourself.

There have even been one or two training camps where I haven't prepared as well as I should have done. The most memorable of these was when I fought a twelve-round contest against an opponent I won't name. The stakes were fairly big at the time, but that didn't stop me from having a drink during the build-up, even though the guy I was fighting had a solid record. The night before our press conference I went out until four in the morning. I then rocked up hungover and told my opponent what I was going to do to him. I stuck to my word too, knocking the dosser out cold when the contest took place. That is the story of my life. There are plenty of fighters that are fitter than me. They can run faster and even punch harder than me. They just can't fight or live like me. And that is their undoing.

CHAPTER EIGHT

LIONHEART

The first press conference for the fight was scheduled for 1 March 2022 at Wembley, but, as the date approached, I was told that Whyte wasn't planning on showing up. Some contractual bollocks had been rumbling on for a while — things I don't involve myself in — regarding Whyte's pay and various other details. I was informed by my promoter that his camp had even demanded a private jet. There were also requests that his photograph be taken off the poster when, really, I was helping him towards a massive payday.

When his no-show was eventually confirmed, Frank Warren went to town. 'I've never heard of anything like it in my life,' he said. 'I've never heard of a fighter not showing up for a press conference for a big fight. He's getting eight times more than Tyson got to fight Klitschko. *Eight times more!* It's more than Anthony Joshua got paid to fight Charles Martin [for his IBF title shot]. He's getting more than Oleksandr Usyk got to fight Joshua. Champions bank on themselves to win. You win the title, you get the money.'

By not showing his face, Whyte had waved a little white

flag. Not that it made a blind bit of difference to me; I was the big draw and could have shifted those 94,000 seats by wrestling my own shadow. But by running away, Whyte was about to miss out on what I think is one of the best parts of the show: *the hype circus*. I've always found it a laugh, especially the big interviews, the TV studios and the photo shoots. Holding court with the world's media is all part of The Gypsy King package and if Whyte didn't want to play the game, then that was up to him. I did though. When the questions started flying around, I let him have it, double barrelled, with no mercy.

Boom! Knockdown #1: 'It's fear. It's terror. It's all of the above. I don't blame him for not being here today, because if he was here, I'd have probably stretched him at the press conference . . . I beat men like him seven days a week and 62 times on a Sunday.'

Boom! Knockdown #2: 'But I've given him a new name, anyway. He's called Frilly in Whyte Knickers. It's not Dillian Whyte, it's Frilly in Whyte Knickers. Because he's as soft as what it says in the title.'

Boom! Knockdown #3: 'There's not even one per cent doubt I'm going to annihilate Dillian Whyte. Even when I've been a heavy underdog, I've never had [the thought] I'm losing. That's my biggest asset, confidence. At this, the latter end of my career, long in the tooth as I am, I'm nearly thirty-four years old, I would never, never let that go away from me. I have to be supremely confident in my own ability, which I am. I believe I can beat Dillian Whyte with one hand tied behind my back and one foot off the floor.'

More than anything, I felt disappointed in Whyte's no-show — not for me, or the fans, but for him. We were about to fight at Wembley Stadium in front of a record crowd for a European boxing match. The last heavyweight contest to grab the attention of the British public in such a way was probably Frank Bruno v Lennox Lewis at Cardiff Arms Park in 1993. No matter what happened on the night, Whyte was set to be a part of sporting history and at some point, when his kids and grandkids were going through the history books, or some old magazines to learn about the time their dad had taken on Tyson Fury, in his prime, they were going to be left with one or two questions . . .

Couldn't you have said something?
Was it really just about the money for you?
Where are the photos and the interviews?

I understand how important it is to be a part of the circus, having earned my unofficial Masters Degree in boxing. You could say I am a doctor of the sport; I know it inside out, round and round, from the beginning to the end. I also have a good memory for stats and records, and over the years I have made a point of researching the legends. Sadly, a lot of my rivals seem to show very little interest in the subject. To them, boxing is nothing more than a way of making a few quid – I don't think Dillian Whyte could name the top five heavyweight champions if I asked him – but I've been built differently. Studying the greats of boxing has taught me what I can and can't do in and around a fight. Knowledge gives me power and as a result I know how to bend and twist the rules to my advantage.

This thirst for information began when I was a kid. *Boxing News*, the weekly magazine, came out on Thursdays and I would be down to the newsagents for a copy every week. (This was just before the internet was born so there were no online boxing sites to go through.) On Sundays I'd head to the car boot sales looking for boxing books, videos and other magazines. I'd buy up bags and bags of VHS tapes, each one with recordings of old fights and new fights; heavyweight champs, middleweight champs and featherweight champs; contests in black and white and contests in colour. Once the internet showed up and YouTube became a thing, I spent hours studying the old timers. I loved every second of it.

That wasn't all. There were books to read, tons of them, like the one you're holding now, and I loved assessing the warriors from the 1920s and 1930s. I wanted to know about their opponents, when and where they fought and how they'd won their titles. Then there were the biographies of Muhammad Ali, Jack Dempsey, James J. Jeffries and George Foreman and I got a buzz learning about their lives outside of the ring as well as their battles inside it. I even loved the *Guinness Book of World Records* and every time a new edition was published I checked out the latest stats. My hunch was that the more info I could pack in, the better I would become at boxing. Education and the ability to use it is what separates humans from the animal kingdom. More importantly, when you really understood the events of the past, you can have a massive impact on the future.

I apply this same thirst for information to my opponents whenever a fight is announced. I like figuring out what makes them tick. I research their motivations. I look at their past bouts and how they fought. I even assess where they come from and how they'd arrived at a point where they were considered good enough to fight at my level. Then I jump into *their* opponents' records to build up a 360-degree picture. By the time the latest challenger has stepped into my world – one in which I've trained like a lunatic, night and day, so I can be ready to beat them up and take them home – they are set for a harsh taste of reality.

Dillian Whyte was no exception.

I have always fancied my chances against high-ranking contenders like Whyte because when it comes to fighting the better standard of opponent, I find it is much easier to knock them out. Well, that's been the case for me at least; for a lot of boxers it is the other way around. Promising new fighters tend to put everyone down during the early stages of their careers because they aren't being lined up against powerful rivals; they are often coming up against journeymen punch bags or blokes who are well past their prime. But as those same up-and-coming fighters progress and the quality of their opponents improves, they find the KOs get harder to come by. It had happened to everyone from Mike Tyson to Anthony Joshua. So far, I'd avoided that pitfall.

In fact, I had annihilated a lot of my opponents because I was able to maintain my power into the later rounds of a fight, building momentum for when it really counted. In my previous four bouts I'd enjoyed one knockout (Deontay Wilder, 2021, eleventh round), two technical knockouts (Deontay Wilder, 2020, seventh round; Tom Schwarz, 2019, second round) and a unanimous decision (Otto Wallin, 2019, twelve rounds). Dillian Whyte, while not quite in the same category as a Wilder, was still a serious test, but I fancied my chances of knocking him out too, though I seemed to be in the minority. A lot of people laughed when I told them my hope in the Wembley build-up. Even my then mate, Derek Chisora doubted I could do it.

'I'm willing to put my house on him knocking Tyson Fury out,' he said, favouring Whyte.

But I knew different. History was on my side and Chisora was about to be homeless.

· · ·

On fight night, Wembley Stadium roared. I stepped away from the throne that had carried me through the crowds. Then I ran to the ropes and jumped inside, where I clocked the look in Dillian Whyte's eyes. He was terrified, like he'd just caught a glimpse of The Grim Reaper, even though he had twenty-eight victories in thirty fights to his name. I'd not seen Whyte in the ring since around 2013 from our sparring days, and the expression on his face told me he was remembering some things, one of them probably being: 'Wow, he really is big with no top on.' He didn't fancy the scrap, it was obvious. Whyte was waiting to be knocked out.

I've won a number of fights without even laying a glove on an opponent in that way, having freaked them out before the very first bell. Some of the blokes I fought on the way up (and then during my comeback) had never been involved in big-time boxing. One or two of them might have had the occasional stadium meeting as part of the undercard, with 15,000 or 20,000 people in the crowd, but coming up against me was an altogether different experience. They were clashing with The Big Dog and the eyes of the world's media were suddenly trained upon them. They had to deal with the hype and the noise of British and American TV. But that's what I bring to the table as a showman, which is daunting for a fighter that isn't as experienced in the way of the game. It's a bit like trying to swim the Atlantic having only done a few lengths of a leisure centre pool.

My trick is to add to my opponents' suffering. I like twisting the knife by saying: 'Welcome to big-league boxing. You're either going to sink or swim.'

I remember Wladimir Klitschko had tried to pull a similar stunt when we'd fought in 2015. 'First time on the big stage?' he said.

But he was messing with the wrong bloke. 'Yeah. But I was made for this. It's my destiny.'

Whyte was no novice though, I could tell that from his record. He'd previously fought at the O2 Arena against the likes of Anthony Joshua, Derek Chisora and Oscar Rivas. But he'd not appeared at the big, glitzy US arenas in Vegas or New York, and Wembley Stadium was on a whole other level. This was 94,000 people and the atmosphere was more like an Oasis gig from back in the day than a sporting event. It wouldn't have helped that he'd need to nail me to the floor if he was to have any hope of winning.

As the first bell rang out, I focused on a battle plan that had been devised with SugarHill in Morecambe. The aim was to bide my time and show patience. All I needed was one opportunity; an opening in which I could land a knockout punch and finish the fight. I even said to SugarHill beforehand, 'This will only go on for as long as I want it to. As soon as I hit him with a proper punch, a detonation, that'll be it.' A display of this kind wasn't exactly what most experts had been anticipating. Given Dillian Whyte's rep as a tough opponent, the expectation was for a slugfest, a war of attrition that lasted the full twelve rounds, with me winning on points. The alternative assumption was for Whyte to stop me late on, roughing me up as he went. What hadn't yet been revealed was that SugarHill had primed me to smash Whyte with a series of perfectly timed monster punches to the face. My powerful fists, wrapped in those St George's Cross gloves, were going to be his biggest test.

Whyte came out southpaw in the first. That was a surprise, he was an orthodox fighter, but I knew not to let his tactical shift throw me off. This was a boxing match, plain and simple, it wasn't rocket science and I'd seen it all before. A fighter was either going to come out southpaw or orthodox, and I had the ways and means of dealing with both. Likewise, there were really only four or five punches* to worry about and I only needed to see them once in an opponent to get the gist of what each one was about. Actually, the only variation in a contest comes from the physique of the other fella, he is either going to be bigger, smaller,

---

* My five main punches are as follows: 1) The jab, the best punch there is. I'm right-handed, so this is a straight shot with the left that comes from below and behind my chest. Everything happens off the back of the jab. 2) The straight right. *My power punch.* 3) The left hook. I normally throw it after a jab-right hand combination. 4) The right hook. I get a lot of power with this one. 5) The uppercut. I like to apply these to the body as well as to the head.

slower or quicker than me and the attitude in every fighter I have ever faced is the same: their hope is to knock me out because it is the only way to handle someone of my size. Funny, nobody has ever managed it, other than an anaesthetist or two.

My first punch was a jab, as always – a left-hander to Whyte's face. Beyond that, the first two rounds were fairly cagey affairs as both of us felt one another out. But everything changed after the third: Whyte was struggling, he was there for the taking, and I'd spotted him panting in his corner at the break, whereas my lungs had felt strong and full. His movement was slowing too. In the fourth I slung out a series of jabs and searching hooks and there was nothing he could do to evade them. Whyte had become a pain magnet. Everything I threw was landing.

It's only a matter of time before you do something spectacular here, I thought.

Then I sent hooks down both sides. His right was clearly the weakest point.

That's where I'm going to take him.

But as I looked again, I began to wonder. *Has Whyte spotted my angle of attack?*

I've *seen* it, I thought. *But has* he *seen me see it?*

Timing was everything in a war like this. Although my opponent was obviously vulnerable, there was no point in me playing up to the crowd, or toying with him like a mouse. It wasn't in my thinking to do that anyway and when fighting a bloke of Whyte's size it was very import-ant to tread carefully. He could easily send a strong punch down my throat and knock me to the canvas, no matter how exposed he might have been at the time. My priority was to get the job done, with no messing around, but I had to strike at the right time. Moving too early might lead me into unloading my tank ahead of time, and if the gamble didn't pay off, I'd have to see the rest of the fight out while running on empty. In that time, Whyte might recover or find his second wind.

I waited for a little longer and then . . .

Crack! In the fifth I hit him with a left hook to the body, slipping inside and breaking him with the shot. He was hurting. I could tell because his arms dropped immediately.

'I've just hurt The Bodysnatcher with a left hook to the body,' I said. 'Are you hurting, Bodysnatcher?'

Whyte grimaced through his gumshield. 'I am,' he mumbled.

I couldn't believe what I was hearing. *He'd admitted it.* 'Right then, you're going to get some more now . . .'

I took my time and picked the strikes, snapping Whyte's head back again, waiting for his weaker side to open up for the perfect bomb. The big right was the only thing left in his locker at that point. He was swinging it wildly and missing by miles.

I laughed at him. 'You think that's ever going to hit me? You must be joking.'

Then, in the sixth, I saw my moment.

Sod it, I thought, *If he's seen me see it, he knows . . . But I'm going in anyway, and . . .*

Pow!

I caught Whyte with the jab, firing a St George's Cross clean from the back of my chest. It must have tenderised the right side of his head. The other glove then pulverised him with a sledgehammer right, an uppercut. The hit was so powerful that one of Whyte's teeth was smacked clean out – anyone watching on the telly would have seen a little white spot spiralling up into the air in slow motion – and it was all too much for him. Whyte collapsed backwards like a demolished tower block folding in on itself and even though he hadn't been knocked unconscious, the ref had seen enough. As Whyte rose to his feet and tottered across the canvas, the fight was stopped. Technical knockout.

A crowd mobbed me. Title belts were wrapped around my shoulders. I saw SugarHill, I saw Paris. But I was wandering over to Whyte. I hugged him and gave him a little kiss.

'I believe you're going to be a world champion one day,' I said. 'But you didn't fight a world champion tonight. You fought a legend in the game. A legend who can't be beat.'

•   •   •

Boxing isn't my entire world. The reality is that I'm a husband, a dad, a son, a brother and an uncle. My family are my armour. Paris and my six beautiful kids are always in my thoughts because they're so precious to me.

Wherever I've lived, or whatever I've been doing, the Traveller values have stuck with me.

[LEFT AND BOTTOM] I'm not unfamiliar with the caravan lifestyle. When I married Paris, we stayed in one for a couple of years while our house was being done up. Here I am filming my ITV show.

The Fury boys have been there to support me throughout my life.

[BELOW]
With Tommy, SugarHill, Hughie and Shane.

[BELOW]
With my brother Tommy.

I was just sixteen
when I met Paris.

Seventeen years later and we're still going strong. The success would
feel pointless if I didn't have her and my six children at my side.

My dad and my uncles provided me with the tools to become a top boxer. My dad has turned into one of my best mates and these days we train together, eat together and argue like cat and bloody dog together. He's nearly sixty now, but he'll run alongside me every morning on a daily jog.

@gypsyjohnfury

@gypsyjohnfury

@gypsyjohnfury

[TOP] SugarHill, with his positive energy and incredible boxing knowledge, has become a part of the furniture. When we first met before *Fury v Wilder II*, he was quiet and shy. But having hung around The Gypsy King crowd for a while, he's morphed into a fucking animal. I've created a monster.

[LEFT] Me with SugarHill, my trainer Kristian Blacklock and my gym partner, the featherweight, Isaac Lowe.

Interesting fact: when I sang 'American Pie' to 94,000 in Wembley Stadium, that meant I'd played to more people at the national stadium than bloody Ed Sheeran, and he is a bona fide pop legend.

Me with my singing partner, Robbie Williams.

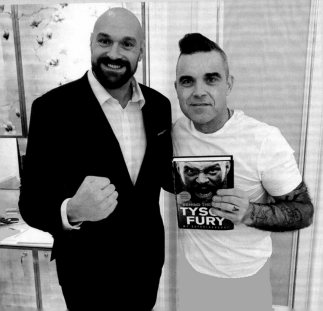

I took the mic and sang to 94,000 people. Then I told the world what was on my mind.

'This might be the final curtain for The Gypsy King,' I said. 'I've spent a lot of time on the road. I've been away [from my family] for a long time.'

There was no party that night. Rather than racking up a huge nightclub bar tab, we drove from Wembley to our Letchmore Heath hotel, only stopping at a petrol station to buy a packet of sweets and a four-pack of beer – one for me, one for Dad, one for Tommy and one for SugarHill. By the time we arrived back at base camp, everyone was shattered. I ordered a delivery pizza that never showed and went to bed, hungry but satisfied, and when I woke the following morning and looked from my window I saw a lone figure sitting on a bench in the hotel garden. *Was he drinking from a bottle of whisky?* I checked my watch. It was 7am.

Bit early, I thought. Then when I looked again, I realised the bloke on the bench was SugarHill.

I stuck my head out of the window. 'What are you doing?'

SugarHill turned and waved the bottle at me. 'I'm celebrating,' he said. 'We didn't do it last night, so I've started this morning.'

'Right. Hold tight, pal. I'm coming down.'

Whisky has never been my thing, I wasn't exactly a fan of shorts either, so as I got myself together I took a couple of beers from the mini bar and joined SugarHill for a weird moment of reflection on that hotel garden bench. It was pretty serene. He'd found a quiet spot in front of a pond. I sat down next to him and cracked open the first drink.

SugarHill nodded and we toasted, our bottles clinking. 'You calmed down, man?' he said.

'Nah, it takes me a while to get back to normal. Probably about two weeks because I've been on such a high, gearing up for the fight. The adrenaline's been pumping all that time and now I've got in there, done the job, I'm still ecstatic. I've got to go from the buzz of winning in front of that crowd last night, Wembley Stadium, to doing the school run with the kids in Morecambe, or going to the shops and back.'

I took a swig of beer. 'And with every high, there's a bigger low ...'

'A low?'

'Yeah,' I said. 'I get depressed after these fights. Instead of being on a high, I'm often down for a few days, maybe a week, and I don't want to be speaking to people. I don't want to be going out in public. I'll just stay at home and do a little bit of training in the gym and just, you know, take some time, some R and R for myself.'

The R and R, I knew, would soon turn into a very different schedule comprising regular tasks to fill my day. I understood that it was important for me to stay occupied because not doing so would only put my mental health at risk. And I would keep exercising. In the build-up to my last few fights it hadn't been the competition that had kept me straight, it was the dedication and effort beforehand. Even though the Whyte fight was done and there was a chance I might be leaving the sport, my plan was to train as if there was still a world heavyweight championship bout to prepare for.

'Can I be honest with you?' I said. 'I don't really go anywhere. I've become like a recluse, a hermit. When I'm not training for a fight, I do exactly the same thing, seven days a week. People think I live this big, extravagant lifestyle, but that's not what it's like to be me. In the week I'll pay the bills, pick up the kids, get my hair cut and take the car to be washed and valeted. On the weekend, I'll take Paris out for a date night or go to the park with the kids.'

It was highly likely that the rest of my time was going to be mapped out in much the same way, unless I decided otherwise. That was OK though, because towards the end of my second career, I understood exactly who and what I was. Yes, I was still Tyson Fury, undefeated heavyweight champion of the world, HMS *I Don't Give A Crap*'s determined admiral, and the greatest fighter of a generation. But I was also a man growing tired of the trappings and the temptations of a life lived in the limelight. My priorities were changing. Now I wanted to be physically fit and emotionally healthy for both my family and myself. By doing the first, I could pretty much guarantee the second, while hopefully calming the dark thoughts I'd experienced during my breakdown and beyond.

I cracked open another beer.

Cheers.

So this was it: the first day of my new life. A routine of domestic chores and hardcore training – maybe for another fight, maybe not – with the occasional chat with Jesus to help keep my demons at bay. Although it sounded mundane, I honestly couldn't have been any happier. I finished my beers; SugarHill finished his whisky. Then we rallied the others at the hotel.

When opening time came around, everybody went to the pub.

PART TWO

ANGELS AND
DEMONS

CHAPTER NINE

SON

I had so much to take in from those blurred moments at the close of *Fury v Whyte*: the lights; the noise; the punch that felled him. There was also the fourteen-year-old boy, Marshall Janson, who I'd invited into the ring afterwards. The kid had lost his hands and legs to meningitis and after meeting up at one of my training camp days, I'd promised Marshall he could join me on the canvas once the fight was done. I heard he later told people that I was *well cool*. Marshall, mate, if you're reading this a) the feeling's mutual, and b) sorry about some of the language in this book.

Most of all, I remember the expression on my dad's face. Framed under the Wembley lights, he looked more like an oil painting than a person. He was full of pride, smiling like the Cheshire Cat, which is everything a son wants to witness in their father, especially as it hasn't always been that way for us. Dad being beside me in the ring was a rarity. For large chunks of my career he wasn't allowed to travel to America, having been sentenced to eleven years in prison for getting involved in a fight in

2011*. Instead he watched all of my US contests on the telly as I emerged victorious from the Wilder trilogy and demolished challengers like Seferi during my comeback.

The time apart was tough. Dad went inside on the eve of my fourteenth professional bout, against the then unbeaten Brazilian, Marcelo Luiz Nascimento, and the news of his sentence was devastating. At one point, during the build-up, I became so down about it all that I even considered jacking in the sport altogether. Dad was having a tougher time of it though. Being stuck in prison was hard enough, but watching me rise to prominence, while defeating the likes of Derek Chisora, caused him to feel helpless, especially as there was no way for him to provide any real-time support. After all that, seeing his son defend the world heavyweight title in front of a heaving Wembley Stadium must have felt amazing.

A quick note before I press on. You won't hear a lot about my mum in these pages because she's not a public person, she's never really had any sort of involvement in my boxing career (as I've mentioned elsewhere, she couldn't bring herself to watch me fight; it terrified her). But she was always incredibly supportive and kind when I was growing up. Dad, on the other hand, has turned into

---

* He was released in 2015, the year of my world championship title fight against Wladimir Klitschko.

one of my best mates and these days we train together, eat together, and argue like cat and bloody dog together. He's nearly sixty now, but he'll run alongside me every morning on a daily jog. It's during those moments where I most feel like I've won in life, our feet pounding the floor as father and son.

At the start of my career Dad was a source of knowledge, and it's no secret that he has a boxing story of his own. Before I was born on 12 August 1988, 'Gypsy' John Fury was a pro heavyweight, taking on the likes of Henry Akinwande, who was then in the early stages of his career, but would later go on to represent Great Britain in the 1998 Olympic Games in Seoul. (Akinwande also won the WBO heavyweight title in 1996 and the European heavyweight title in 1993, so he was no slouch.) Dad was knocked out after three rounds in that one, but over a short career, he won eight, lost four, and drew one. What he lacked in technique was more than made up for with a serious amount of determination.

'Once I'd got going, I'd not stop swinging until they were out cold,' he said once. 'I'd not come up for air. Afterwards, shake hands and on to the next one.'

I was too young to have seen my dad fight, but as a teenager I got to watch him up close whenever he worked a punch bag in the garden shed. At that time my obsession with boxing was growing, as it was for my younger brother Shane. Seeing Dad's passion for training only lobbed more fuel on the fire and we wanted to run, lift weights and hit things like he did. A pivotal story from this time – which I've told before but want to expand on here – took place when I was fourteen. I had watched a couple of Dad's fights on video and called him out for not being so good. He'd been pounding away in the shed at the time, working up a sweat, and I don't think he was too happy about the criticism.

'Alright then,' he said, taking off his gloves and handing them over. 'Let's see what *you've* got.'

I pulled them on, all excited, thinking he was going to show me around the bag. Instead he took me outside.

'Hit me in the body,' he said.

I really wasn't sure what to make of that. *I didn't want to properly punch him.* 'I'm not hitting you in the body,' I said.

'Yes you are,' he snapped. 'Hit me in the guts.'

I didn't need to be told twice. When Dad wanted me to do something, I did it, no chatting back. The same went for all my brothers. Stepping forwards, I wound up a hammer punch that exploded into his side, breaking three ribs. I'd shocked him, no doubt, and Dad came back at me to spar, but after a while he was forced to sit down. With one punch I'd done a man that had taken some heavy punishment as a professional fighter. Apparently not even Henry Akinwande had hurt him quite as badly.

'Yeah, you can definitely fight,' he wheezed. 'Crack on.'

At that stage in life I knew exactly what I wanted to become (the world's greatest heavyweight) and what was needed to get me there (training, training, training). Everyone else could see it too, especially Dad, but from time to time he'd try to discourage me from taking the sport overly seriously.

'Don't bother doing this,' he'd say. 'It's a mug's job.'

That had a lot to do with the fact that Dad was a journeyman fighter. Sometimes he was placed into a bout with next to no chance of winning, so I suppose he didn't want the same experience for me. But no way was I paying any attention to that, or anyone else that didn't believe in my ambition or talents. From a young age I learned a lot about the dream-crushers and naysayers. They were the people that told me I couldn't, when I could, and a lot of them reckoned I was dreaming – to them I was just a kid living in a fantasy land. And yet whenever I asked them about the championships fights *they'd* won, or got them to name the belts *they'd* lifted, the response was always the same. *Sweet bollocks-all.* In the end, the pessimistic comments pinged away from me like water off a duck's back and I became increasingly determined to give everyone the big middle finger. Even as a kid, Tyson Fury did whatever he wanted. The only person I had to keep happy back then was me, and that same attitude applies today.*

As I got older it became clear that people view champion boxers in much the same way in which they view the prime minister, or the manager of the England football team. *Everyone thinks they know better*. The amount of times I've had random people approach me in the street to tell me some tactic I should be using to knock over a fighter like Dillian Whyte or Deontay Wilder is unbelievable.

'You should move this way,' they'd say. 'You should punch that way.'

'Oh right. Thanks,' I'd think. 'You're a cabbie/pub landlord/traffic warden from Sheffield, I'm the heavyweight champ . . . But I should take your advice?'†

As with the people I ignored while growing up, most of the 'helpful' info I have been given as a pro boxer has been rejected – apart from one or two things that Dad told me when I was younger. Having said that, he discouraged me from wedding Paris.

---

* Correction: The only other person I've ever had to make happy has been Paris. If she's happy, I'm happy, and on to a good 'un.
† I'm kidding, I don't mind you offering me advice on my jab in the street if you want. I'm still waiting for the magic tip, though.

He said, 'You can't be married and be a professional boxer.'

Eh? 'Why not?'

'Because once you're married you won't put your full attention into it. You'll have responsibilities. You'll have bills to pay. You'll have to look after this person. You'll have to do that and you'll have to do this . . .'

Did I listen to him? Hell, no, I didn't.

I was also told not to drink, smoke, or take drugs. Well, I drank beer, I smoked a cigarette and at the height of my mental breakdown, I tried cocaine. I regret the last one for sure, but in making those mistakes I learned some important lessons, so there was value in the experience. I also recall someone telling me to invest in Bitcoin years before it exploded in price. Good tip. *Did I listen?* Of course not; unfortunately I bought a car instead, though I got plenty of value from that too. The bottom line is this: it's human nature to defy other people's suggestions. It's why Adam and Eve ate that apple in the Garden of Eden and why the world is the way it is today.

If there were one piece of advice I wish I *had* heard during my early days as a fighter, it would be this: business and family just don't mix. The Notorious B.I.G. had even summed the theory up in his track, 'Ten Crack Commandments', when he explained how it was a good move to keep your family and business apart, because mixing them led to trouble. While Dad had got me started in the sport, and I appreciated it, at different stages my uncles Hughie and Peter trained me and there was friction and plenty of upset, all of it caused by boxing.

I even had a falling out with my dad during the build-up to the first Deontay Wilder fight, though it was relatively short-lived. Suddenly he was stressed out that I might get myself badly hurt, which wasn't the best thing to say to a person on the eve of going into the ring with one of the deadliest punchers on the planet. In the end he stopped talking to me for six or seven weeks. I cracked on, like he'd told me to after that first-ever punch, because when people don't believe in me it is their problem, not mine. I am there to do a job, nothing more, nothing less.

In the end, Dad and me patched up our differences and I emerged from those three Wilder fights victorious and reborn. As always, I'd kept my own counsel, because it has served me so well over the years. Like Frank Warren and fight promotion: what Tyson Fury doesn't know about knocking people out isn't worth knowing.

●　●　●

Despite my professional experience and boxing know-how, Dad was still able to deliver a few helpful lessons when

I made my way in the professional game. The main one focused on work ethic and money because Dad was a real powerhouse and always very busy. When I was little he was always flat-out working, seven days a week, so he could earn a few quid and pay the bills. In doing so, the Fury kids had a roof over our heads and we were able to eat and live well.

As with boxing, I received an early education in the value of a hard day's graft when I was pulled out of school around the age of ten or eleven, which was a common occurrence in Traveller families. Not that it affected me negatively. I could have studied until the age of 110 years old and not been as successful as I am now. That said, I know at the time I was enjoying school life, even though I wasn't going to receive an education in boxing during PE lessons, and I had no involvement in the decision to leave – I packed up one summer and never went back. But shortly afterwards, I began working with Dad and together we sold second-hand cars. From there he taught me that if I could do a job myself, rather than relying on others to do it for me, I'd become really independent really fast.

It was tips like these that set me up for life. I might not have received a traditional education. I can't tell you much about the Three Rs – reading, 'riting, 'rithmatic – but by working so hard and from such a young age I developed a very good level of street sense and emotional intelligence. This has meant that later on in life I've been able to count up a million quid when required; I've done a lucrative deal with Netflix, on my own, without lawyers; and I've had it in me to meet with the head of ESPN and settle a huge contract in seconds.

I'll never forget my first car sale. I was just out of school and our next-door neighbour had an old Renault in his garden, so I made him an offer of £50. Not long afterwards, I managed to shift it for £250. Seeing a 400 per cent profit felt amazing.

'I'm so proud that you've done that, son,' said Dad, afterwards.

And before long I was involved in more buying, more selling. As I settled trade after trade, I understood how to spot a bargain, and how to sniff out a dud. I quickly realised that no matter what the commodity was – cars, bricks, or properties – the concept was always the same. A successful trader bought at one price, improved the item, and then shifted it for profit.

When I was in my teens, and my boxing obsession had really taken root, I came to understand the value of physically hard effort, and for eight hours a day I worked as a manual labourer, earning £40, grinding like a tank, lifting bricks while getting battered and messed up. It helped to make me unbreakable and I always went to the boxing gym straight afterwards so I could get even more battered and messed up. The effort was hard, but satisfying, and having so many different jobs before my life as a pro fighter allowed me to take in the view from both sides of the fence – I was able to appreciate the emotional rewards that arrived with working hard.

At some moment in time, while I was carrying a stack of bricks probably, Dad even said to me: 'One pound of your own is worth fifty quid of somebody else's.'

What do you mean by that?

'Tyson, if you've got a car, an old Corsa and it's falling to bits, but you've earned that Corsa ... *Be proud of it.* Everything you've had to work your bollocks off for, you'll appreciate, no matter what it is. Because the lad who's driving his dad's Porsche: guess what? He didn't earn that, so he can't be proud of it.'

That advice stuck with me. But I was always financially savvy and as a kid I tried to save as much of my money as I could. That way I would feel as if I'd earned my rewards, whatever they were. I didn't want to buy things on credit. I also knew it was far better to be earning a small amount and saving a chunk of it, than earning a lot and blowing it all. Fast-forward ten years, when the cash was rolling in and I was making my fame and fortune as the heavyweight champion of the world, I still only spent what I'd already earned. I didn't waste it on crap either, or stuff I wasn't going to appreciate.

I think I'm different to a lot of boxers, the fighters who

haven't worked at anything else in their lives, other than pursuing the goal of becoming a supreme athlete. Those fighters might only know the gym, or the boxing ring, so when their bank accounts start to bulge with unbelievable numbers, knowing what to do with it all can become a massive problem. Some of them blow it on rubbish, or on people that don't care about their welfare. But I've never come close to behaving the same way because I've learned the truth about fame and money. The idea that it will bring me joy is the biggest lie ever and there is no true pleasure in it. The buzz wears off after only a few minutes, whereas proper happiness innately comes from within.

• • •

The other important lesson that Dad delivered involved friendship and the importance of keeping a tight circle around me. 'A mate that wants you to change, for whatever reason, isn't a genuine person,' he said. As my career has started to draw to a close, I am still mixing with the same people that I've been hanging around with for some twenty years. One of them is a roofer; another does windows and conservatories; there is a boxer in the group and I've known him since I was a kid. Finally there is a pal I've been tight with since the age of thirteen. These people accepted the real me, way before I was famous.

As for whether professional boxers hang out together, or chat from time to time, I don't think that happens too much – at least not in my experience. Most of us have our own mates and our own friendship circles to mix in. That's not to say I don't have pals in the sport. I've become really close with the former WBO heavyweight champion, Joseph Parker. He comes up to the gym and we train together, so we've got to know each other well. Another friend is the featherweight, Isaac Lowe, who has been a gym partner for several years. Aside from these guys there are also some good relationships to be found in the trainers I've worked with, like SugarHill, of course.

I am happy with having people like this around. As for the rest of it, I'm just not that interested, and I have certainly never felt impressed by celebrity. Whenever a rich or famous individual comes into my life, I treat them as an associate, even though they might be a great person. My attitude: *I don't know them. I didn't know them while I was growing up. I didn't know them when I wasn't anything. So why would I want to really know them when I'm a somebody?* That's not to say that I don't meet genuine people along the way, because life is like a train journey. People get on. People get off. And you never knew who is going to be on the platform when you arrive at somewhere new.

One of those characters is Ed Sheeran, who I once met

backstage at a Manchester gig. After chatting for around an hour and a half, I realised we are both very similar in character. Ed is grounded, he has nothing in the way of an entourage – his road manager is his best mate and everyone around him appears to be somebody that he's grown up with. From what I can tell, his idea of happiness is a night in the local boozer with a packet of crisps and a pint, drinking alongside his pals, with no hangers on. I can appreciate the value in that.

As for entourages, *no thanks*. I've never had one in my life because the idea of having bag-carriers about me – or do-gooders and tappers-on-the-backers for that matter – doesn't make any sense. I like to carry my own bag. I don't need people to kiss my arse. I certainly don't need to be told how good I am. *I know how good I am.* The only entourage I've had during a training camp or in the build-up to a fight was a group featuring my trainers and corner crew, and my family, plus one or two of my close friends that have been there from the beginning. Again, I'm different in this respect. I even got into a heated discussion with Deontay Wilder about it on the eve of one of our fights. I noticed that he had all these people around him, so I gave it to him, big time.

'You're going to end up broke!' I said. 'Back where you started. One of us ain't right: you've got all these people around you, all this jewellery on, these sparkling diamonds, you've got all this glitz and glamour. And you've got all these idiots round you. Bag-carriers. Look at you, you're a classless man.'

'Classless?' he snapped. 'If you call this classless, I'll be classless any day.'

'OK. Let's meet up in ten years when it's all over and we'll see if you've got any money left. Then we'll see if any of these pricks are still hanging around you . . .'

Listen, I like company as much as the next person. I enjoy having friends around me all the time. Even the greatest person who ever lived, Jesus Christ, had twelve people in his corner. That's because mankind needs conversation, hence why God made two instead of one. But I'm all about mixing with mates who are full of loyalty and love, characters that won't do a runner when the good times stop rolling. I want pals that will be there through thick and thin, but those people are very hard to find in my line of work. Sure, I could have had loads of film director friends, footballer friends, or pop star friends. But how many of them want to be friends with me, the person, rather than with Tyson Fury, the boxer?

Sadly, that's how I started in the beginning. In the early days I ignored Dad's advice and sometimes allowed certain people to come on board, characters that didn't know me from before. We went on big nights out together; we were seen around town together, but I was used and abused by them and I was chucked away in 2015 when my man-of-the-moment status seemed to be over. That was an important reality check and it will never happen again. These days I appreciate the true value of friendships. That's why I'd much rather go running with Gypsy John than sip champagne with the world's most famous.

CHAPTER TEN

THE RIGHT SIDE OF THE TRACKS

If ever a Hollywood director fancied making another boxing film in the style of *Rocky*, I doubt they'd look to my childhood for inspiration. I'm very different to the movie clichés: that angry, detached kid brought up on the wrong side of the tracks, channelling his rage in a decrepit backstreet gym while sparring with bums and dossers. Growing up was fun, a right laugh and I felt safe and cared for all the time. It was for this reason that one or two pundits argued against me making it to the very top during the early phases of my career. *Apparently I hadn't suffered enough.*

This idea was even discussed on the telly when Sky Sports invited me to a round table interview featuring the British heavyweights, Lennox Lewis, Frank Bruno, Anthony Joshua and Scott Welch. Entitled *The Gloves Are Off*, the chat turned to how each of us had started out in the game. Lennox talked about his tough upbringing, Frank and Anthony Joshua had similar stories, and by the sounds of it Scott Welch learned to look after himself while growing up in Great Yarmouth. Boxing had probably been a lifesaver for some of them. But when it came to my story, the angle completely changed. I was twenty-one, full of confidence and keen to put everyone straight.

'I never was in trouble,' I said. 'Never been in trouble in my life. I had everything I ever wanted. I had a good upbringing and I box because I want to box. It's inside me that I want to be a champion. I didn't box because I needed to keep out of trouble. I wasn't forced . . . I was never gonna do anything else apart from boxing.'

What I'd said probably caused some people to doubt my chances of success. *Their attitude?* 'We don't think you'll make world champion because you've got money. Some young fighters out there are struggling to pay the bills and they'll want it more than you . . .'

I hate that kind of mentality, where a person is judged on whether they are going to be successful according to their class, background, gender or colour. Drive would decide my boxing success. If a person is to succeed they have to dedicate their life to the chosen cause – whatever that cause might be. What I knew was that the boxing bull was getting grabbed by the horns; once I'd wrestled him to the ground, I was cutting a fillet steak from the bastard. And no way was Tyson Fury going to listen to the opinions of anyone that didn't really know him.

Looking for trouble was never my thing. The tactic when growing up was to keep myself to myself because I wanted to avoid any bother, though bother seemed to find me. During the first seconds of my very first round in the big wide world, I had to fight hard because I was close to passing away, much like Athena had been during her birth in 2021. My issue was that I'd arrived three months prematurely and weighed a featherweight 1 pound. I died three times, but came back four, and though the doctors didn't fancy my chances of leaving the hospital in one piece, I somehow made it, with a name to match my early struggles.

Tyson Fury.

The title had been my dad's idea because according to him I'd shown the spirit of the ferocious, former heavy-weight champion of the world, Iron Mike. He then went about telling everyone that I was going to be a giant and a champion boxer, and with hindsight he really should have put a bet on. What he didn't know was that my name would become an attention grabber, especially as I rose through the boxing ranks in my late teens. I had the super-hero moniker; people wanted to know whether I had the powers to match, so they were drawn to my fights when-ever I appeared on the card.

I was loved and supported throughout my childhood, and the Fury boys — my three brothers John-Boy, Shane and Hughie, and me — lived in a cottage on a farm in Styal, a small village near Wilmslow in Cheshire, which was famous for housing the Quarry Bank Mill. It was a nice place, and in a way we were fairly secluded. For the most part, the brothers mainly stuck together, though we sometimes hung out with our cousins and one or two close friends. Other than that we stuck close to our dad's side when he wasn't working.

My primary school was tiny; I think there were only eleven kids in my class and one year Prince Charles (or King Charles, as I should now say) showed up to plant a tree — it was that kind of place. Given I was a big boy, I was typically shoved in goal for the school football team, which I liked and I became a Manchester United fan. I enjoyed school too and I fitted in well with the people around me because I was polite. I was raised to conduct myself in a proper manner, I saw myself as a good kid and believed that what went around came around: if you were a good person and worked hard, good things came back to you. But if you were a piece of crap, you could expect payback at some point.

It wasn't all good times. When I was around the age of three, I endured a series of worrying episodes in which I burned up with a very high temperature. Sometimes I became delirious and suffered all sorts of visions as a result — one time I genuinely believed my room had caught fire; on another occasion I became convinced a lion was stalking me as prey. The condition was so bad I was taken to hospital a few times, but nobody could figure out what was wrong with me.

I also experienced depression, though I couldn't understand exactly what it was, or why it was happening. From the age of six, there were times where I felt scared for no apparent reason, or anxious at the thought of being left behind. Whenever I mentioned it to anyone in the family, the general response was: *Oh, Tyson's playing up*, and in the end, I ignored my heavy emotions, keeping them to myself for years. That was a mistake, because it created more and more pressure, like shaking up an unopened bottle of pop. When I eventually cracked the lid later on in life, the explosion made a nasty mess.

These were isolated incidents and for much of the time, growing up in Styal was fun. We had a traditional family set-up for the era – Mum was at home, Dad was at work, and us kids had a real sense of freedom. Fields surrounded our cottage and we would race about the place on bikes, motor-bikes and quad bikes. There was also a forest nearby and I often wandered in there with one of my few mates, Zach, and we'd cycle along cliffs and through streams; we climbed rocky faces and scaled trees – all proper Boy's Own stuff.

We had a sense of wanderlust too. Sometimes, Zach and I would get on a bus or two and travel all the way to Bala in north Wales, just so I could see my cousin, even though it was miles away from home. I had another mate, Justin, who used to live in Lincoln, so we would stay over there, too. The craze back then was to ride about on stainless steel micro scooters and once we'd got to Justin's we'd then scoot and bus another twenty miles to Boston. Having strolled about the place, we'd have a plate of sausage, chips and beans in the local café and then make the journey back.

We were never told off for these adventures, because nobody knew what we were up to. As a kid you could do that kind of thing back then without getting any bother. We were safe. Plus it helped that none of us were cheeky, or gobby, but that was thanks to us watching boxing at home, and later when we started boxing in the gym. We knew what it was like to get punched in the face, so we kept our mouths shut.

• • •

I loved grafting as a kid, and some of my most vivid childhood memories are of my brothers, cousins and me hustling to make a few quid. If I wasn't helping Dad to sell cars during the day, we'd leave the house to earn, sometimes making as much as £100 or £120 between us. No job was too big and for a while we tried our hand at scrap dealing. Whenever it snowed, we'd sweep the village driveways for a fee. Then we'd grab something to eat, walk to the gym and train for a couple of hours. But the money was a happy bonus. The real motivation for doing it was the laughs.

One of the first things we involved ourselves in was chicken breeding and trading, which might sound like a weird hobby for a kid to take up, but when you stripped it all back it was really no different to collecting Pokémon cards, or football stickers. We were surrounded by animals at the cottage, and there were dogs and cats, horses and donkeys, geese and ducks all over the place. Dad also had some chickens, so naturally Shane and I got into them as well. It was crazy times. Our money-making ambitions really ramped up once we'd got into the scrap game. Somebody had the idea that we should cruise about the nearby council estate to collect old appliances. They'd heard that a local junk dealer was buying up old washing machines and toasters for £40 or £50 a ton. Convinced we were on to a winner, us Fury boys spent our days driving around, looking for treasure, chucking whatever we could into the back of the car or van, often getting covered in crap from the inside of a broken oven, or tumble drier. Then we'd sell our haul for as high a price as possible.

Really it was all about making memories. We would roam the streets, giggling our heads off, messing around and cracking jokes. If ever we got bored, one game we used to play was called Hedgehogging. We'd line up and take a run at a neighbour's hedge or bushes, jumping into their garden before being chased away. It was nothing serious, just a little fun and we never did any harm. At the time we

161

didn't realise how good we had it back then and it's only when I recall these stories now that I can see how much of a laugh we had. I tell my kids today that it's important to create good times.

A strong work ethic had been entrenched in the family for generations. My grandmother on my dad's side, Patience, was a grafter (she used to help her dad tarmac the roads as a kid) and whenever I went round there, I would clean her house and run chores. If ever I went on holiday to see my aunt and uncle I would have to earn my time on the beach by picking up rubbish or doing a little manual labour. But that gave me the desire to slog away. In the Netflix movie *Hustle*, Adam Sandler plays a pro basketball scout and he tells his latest prospect that 'obsession is going to beat talent every time.' That's only partly true, because if you're relying on obsession, you'll always be beaten by a person who possesses talent *and* the ability to push themselves to the limit. Luckily, I had both and my willingness to work had been drummed into me as a kid. I was on to a winner.

• • •

I remember overhearing a conversation once where two blokes were discussing Traveller culture.

'How do you know if you are one?' said the first man.

The answer was pretty simple. 'You either are one or you're not. There's nothing more to it.'

As a family, we were Travellers because Mum and Dad had lived as Travellers. That meant my brothers and me were Travellers too – *you are what your parents were*. I've had this conversation with a few people recently and there are certain criteria when deciding who does and who doesn't qualify. For example, if you one day decided to up sticks and live the Traveller lifestyle, you wouldn't officially be classed as one of us. However, if you then raised kids and they lived in the same way, they would be classed as Travellers. It takes a generation to lay down roots.

The reality is that you can't just sign a contract and say, 'Oh I'm a Traveller now.' Or, 'I'm a Gypsy these days . . .' And even if you could, that process has been complicated because law has bunched the different strands of travelling people – like Gypsy, Roma and Traveller – under one umbrella, when in fact we're all very different. And just as it takes a generation to officially become a Traveller, it only takes a generation for a person's connection to the culture to break. So, say a kid was born into a Traveller family and became adopted by a non-Traveller family, they would be considered a Traveller by blood. But if they stopped practising the traditions from our culture, their connection would die away.

That's certainly been the case in some parts of our family.

Dad has some first cousins that haven't lived like Travellers, so our way of living has faded for them. But we definitely lived as Travellers* because I was raised with the traditions, which aren't too dissimilar to the old English way of doing things. The Furys are family-orientated and God-fearing. We are big on moral values. And we always stick together.

Faith played a part and it's always been a big deal to me. My uncle was a preacher and when I was a young kid I would watch him speak in church. My grandfather, Hugh, was a staunch Catholic and he taught me to say, 'In the name of the Father, and of the Son, and of the Holy Ghost. Amen,' as well as a load of prayers. It quickly became a big part of my life; I prayed every night before bed and took to studying the Bible. Listening to all the different opinions on religion was fascinating too because everyone seemed to have a different take on what faith actually is – I realised that we all have varying belief systems and different ways of practising our ideals.

I've stayed close to God throughout my entire life. When I was a young boxer, at around the age of seventeen, I went to Ireland and an old bloke in his eighties came up to me. He said, 'You stay tight to the Big Man Upstairs, son and you'll be alright . . .' And that's what I have tried to do ever since.

* We didn't move around from area to area as kids, but that didn't matter. We didn't actually need to travel to be considered Travellers.

Of course, there have been moments where I've strayed and lived on my own morals rather than His. But that's when I've come unstuck. Each time I've got back with God afterwards and everything has rolled smoothly.

Our home life seemed much more settled than it did for some Travellers. Way before *Grand Designs* had started on the telly, Dad bought our cottage in Styal with the intention of doing it up. The process went on for years and while the work was being completed, the family shifted into a no-frills four-bed static home with a living room and dining room. I was only four years old then, so I can't remember too much about it, but I do remember the flood that hit us several years later, once we'd made Dad's cottage our castle. Off we went, back to the static home again, while extensive repairs took place.

So I wasn't unfamiliar with the caravan lifestyle. Later, when I married Paris, we stayed in one for a couple of years while our house was being done up. But that's the thing about me: I don't care if I live in a castle or a caravan; a bed's a bed and a bog's a bog and it doesn't matter if it is a rickety old seat or a loo carved from gold. To me, the days spent in caravans and static homes were no different to living anywhere else, though I'm not sure why they're such a big deal in the UK holiday market. A caravan costs forty, fifty grand. Then it needs towing to wherever you want to visit. You have to clean it, empty the waste and then pay

£100 a night to stay in a special park. For that amount you'd expect a fortnight's all-inclusive stay in a super fancy, five-star resort abroad.

That said, I do have a caravan that I like to use from time to time. Recently I hitched it to the car and went to the little touring park that's around four doors from where I live in Morecambe Bay. I just pulled in there for a couple of nights with the kids and it was absolutely fantastic. It was close enough to home so that we could collect anything that we might have forgotten and we got takeaways, like fish and chips. Northern seaside towns are famous for their chippies, so we did alright.

Wherever I've lived, or whatever I've been doing, the Traveller values have stuck with me. One of them regards the importance of manners, and Dad always encouraged me to show respect, especially to my elders.

'If an older person comes in the room, you get up and let them sit down,' he said.

I've since carried that attitude with me and habitually give up my seat for a pensioner or a pregnant woman without even thinking about it. I'll help people across the street. If someone's car has conked out on the side of the road, I'll give them a tow, or a push. The same mindset applies to bullies – I feel the need to help the person getting attacked. As a kid, I hated to see people getting picked on and if there was any intimidation happening I always tried to sort it.

If there was a load of people hammering one person and it was nowt to do with me, I'd still jump in and help the victim. I'm not trying to signal to the world about how wonderful I am, I'm just painting a picture of the rules we were taught as Traveller kids. Be polite. Look out for others. Respect your elders.

I'm also telling you all this because there are certain misconceptions about Travellers that are really annoying. Recently, there was an incident in a pub in Morecambe Bay, the home of The Gypsy King. An old man in his seventies wanted to go for a pint with his son-in-law, but when they got to the door, a bouncer blocked their way, even though they weren't causing trouble, or likely to.

'Sorry, guys, no Travellers allowed,' said the bouncer.

The two men couldn't believe it. 'Why, what have *we* done?'

It turned out there had been some trouble with a few Travellers during the previous week. Rather than banning the actual offenders, the brewery had decided to punish the entire community – but not for long. Once word spread about the incident, a 2,000-strong march took place in the area and a protest gathered around the pub. Eventually, the protest's high-profile nature caused the boozer to change their policy. This was hardly a one-off. Before becoming famous, I experienced similar treatment and there were times when my entry to a club or pub was barred – usually on the say-so of the local police, and even though I hadn't done anything personally. It was crazy.

Of course, I get that there are dodgy apples in the Traveller community, as there is in any group – you can't tell me there isn't good and bad in all people. I could go down to one of the more expensive boxes at a fancy racecourse, or a five-star restaurant somewhere and see a bunch of wrong 'uns wreaking havoc. The problem is that when a Traveller or a Gypsy causes a scene, the whole community is judged. They're then painted with the same brush in the fallout.

I don't know whether I've experienced any prejudice in boxing because of my culture, but that's because my career progress has been impossible to stop. Nobody could have blocked my path with politics, or because of some weird issue with my background, even if they had wanted to. Instead, I've earned the right to fight on merit, and I don't care what dosser I'm punching out to move forward. Whoever's standing in my way on the canvas, I'll hit – and hard – because knocking down motherfuckers is my job. Which is bad news for the motherfuckers.

CHAPTER ELEVEN

FIRST BLOOD

My first-ever bout took place in our neighbour's front garden. I was a kid, probably only nine years old and wearing a turquoise Donald Duck tracksuit, when my older brother John-Boy came up with a suggestion.

'Here, do you want to fight the lad from next door?' he said.

Apparently John and the brother of this wannabe fighter had dreamt up a crackpot idea. There was to be a boxing showdown in the street, and like a pair of junior Don Kings they were promoting the younger siblings in what would be their first competitive bout.

'Yeah, why not?' I thought. 'It's only a fight, isn't it?'

I was at the point where watching Dad's training had really fired up my interest, so I happily traipsed round, my trackie bottoms barely held in place by a drawstring waistband. Then I threw a few punches. It was hardly a dramatic introduction to pugilism, but I felt OK when hitting someone else, what with my watching plenty of fights on video and studying the photos in *Boxing News*. In fact, the thing I remember most from the contest was my trousers. They kept drooping down and it soon became a monumental effort to land a blow while holding up my pants with the other hand. Eventually the two older brothers stopped the fight. Why, I'm not sure. I don't even know if anyone was declared a winner or not.

Other than that, I didn't get into any real scraps as a kid, not outside of boxing anyway. I didn't have that kind of personality. I never had an attitude where I wanted to prove myself as being big, or bad, and I didn't have a chip on my shoulder. I also didn't have that aura where people felt as if they wanted to test themselves against me, which I know some people *do* have. When I was interviewed by Piers Morgan he made the point that whenever Lennox Lewis went into a pub, he seemed to get into a fight. I just have never had that experience, even though I've been to some of the roughest places in the world, as well as some of the plushest. That doesn't mean I am the shy and retiring type, or keen to keep my head down in some show of diplomacy. Growing up I was the life and soul of wherever I went, still am, and I've happily walked into a bar topless, or danced on the tables for a laugh. I just never really get started on.

That's a good thing because I'm terrified of punching someone in the face. *Think of the damage I could cause.* One right-hander from me could probably crush a normal, untrained man's skull and I'd probably end up in prison for manslaughter or murder. *No thanks.* If somebody takes a swing at me (and they are lucky enough to land it) I'd flash a grin and say, 'Thank you very much. Shit punch, *prick*.' Then I would ignore them. Really, the consequences of retaliating are too scary to imagine and I've long recognised the truth about combat. The danger is not the man holding the gun; the danger is the man holding the gun who can't control himself. *He's the scary one.* Luckily, I've been brought up to be sensible, and as Frank Warren would confirm, I'm not one for putting my fists into action unless somebody is paying me top dollar.

As kids, my brothers and I tried our hand at boxing, and all with varying degrees of success. Well, apart from Hughie, who is a lot younger than us. John-Boy trained with our dad for a while but couldn't seem to get into it. But Shane and me found a love for the sport at the same time and it quickly came to dominate our lives. One time, after that neighbourhood championship bout, Dad took me up to a gym in Liverpool where he worked out twice a week because he knew I enjoyed watching the fighters as they punched the bags – and each other. At the time, I knew I wanted to take boxing more seriously, and studying other people doing it only added to my enthusiasm. As I grew older, I started sparring a little bit and I even went up against a couple of kids in a gym in Liverpool, when my dad was training. They were twins and pretty handy, but I came out on top. More importantly, I knew that I was very lucky. In boxing I had found the thing I'd wanted to do in life and I was determined to put my heart and soul into it.

• • •

My brothers and I, plus some cousins, were always fighting among ourselves, arguing up and down. Mainly, I hung around with Shane, who was three years my junior — Hughie was too young then and John-Boy was older and already too cool for school. But despite the fact I was younger than some of the boys in the family, I was by far the biggest, and at the age of fourteen I stood at 6 foot 6 and weighed about 15 stone. I looked like a man, but I didn't take advantage of it by trying to buy booze or cigarettes because none of us were interested in any of that. We were training. Our eyes were fixed on becoming top boxers, and if you were working to be a boxer, then drinking and smoking didn't seem very appealing.

I soon joined up with a boxing club. Up until that point, I had no idea there was even one in the area, but when a local lad told Shane and me about the Jimmy Egan Boxing Academy in Wythenshawe, which was around three miles away, we made a decision to join. The pair of us walked all the way there the very next day. I had to pay subs to enter, a quid or something, and almost from the minute

I started being put through my paces, the trainer, Steve Egan – Jimmy's son – became very excited.

I was an orthodox fighter, which meant I jabbed with my left and delivered the big hits with my right. But what was interesting to Steve was the fact that I could avoid a punch just as well as I could throw one. I was agile and nimble on my feet, which was unusual for a boy of my build. I could go into battle with someone and only take a few hits. After one session, Steve had seen enough. He wanted to give me a registration card straightaway. 'That kid over there will be heavyweight champion of the world,' he said to his dad.

Jimmy couldn't believe what he was hearing. 'What? He's just walked in the door—'

'I'm telling you, heavyweights don't move like that.'

He was right, they don't, and I was soon under Steve's tutelage. He taught me how to shift from the orthodox style to southpaw, where a fighter jabs with their right and throws bombs with their left, knowing it would give me an advantage over some of the other competitors in my weight category. He also worked on my speed and I was encouraged to align my quick feet to an armoury of rapid punches. The work would make for good grounding as I progressed.

Everywhere I went, people seemed to notice my talents. One time, I was training at a gym in Doncaster when a

Chinese man came over. He looked me up and down and asked me what I wanted to be.

A boxer.

'Oh yeah? How old are you?'

Seventeen.

The bloke nodded. Then he made an unusual offer. 'Why don't you come to LA with me and we'll get you a contract with the LA Lakers basketball team?'

I wasn't interested. 'Thanks for the suggestion,' I said. 'But my dream is to be heavyweight champion of the world. Not bothered about anything else . . .'

Though Dad taught me one or two boxing skills by holding his hands up (and allowing me to crunch his ribs that one time), Steve was my first proper coach. He put his life and soul into me and for five years, from the age of fourteen, I worked with Steve on combination punching. Then he grounded me and showed me the basics of boxing, which helped me to build a strong foundation for my career.

Steve was a great trainer because he showed me nothing but love and affection, but he also listened to what I was saying, which was important for a kid of my age and we spent a lot of time chatting. But he also kept me nice and reinforced the importance of respect. Steve was kind too: if I'd forgotten my subs money (which really only covered the bills for the gym) he fronted me, and as my career progressed through the amateur ranks, we travelled all over the place together so I could box and spar.

I really put the work in with Steve but I had the talent and dedication to repay his faith. The fact about boxing is that a fighter can be coached to death, but if they haven't got the ability to back it up, no amount of training is going to push them to the top level. So while it was great that Steve was telling me to punch this way, or move that way, the skill and intuition to know when to deliver those moves came from me. I also knew that if a tactic or technique wasn't working then I would have to switch it up, sometimes in the middle of a fight, in order to survive. My time with Steve at Egan's gym was an amazing starting gun for my career, and he delivered one vital piece of advice – a line that chimed with my dad's opinion on graft. *If you're going to work, work hard.*

Now there was a rule to live your life by.

Steve's dad, Jimmy, sadly passed away from cancer a year after I'd first met him, but the club has kept going. It is a community centre really, and has been a fixture in the area for around fifty years. Steve still works with the local kids for free (the club makes their money through the adults), and having dedicated so much time and effort to an unpaid service, I consider him, and his late dad, to be special people. I certainly benefited from their generosity when I was younger, visiting the gym whenever I could, but I soon hit a roadblock as a teenager: because of my size and age there was nobody for me to fight competitively. I was only fourteen, but I'd already been classed as a super heavyweight, albeit a junior one. My problem was that the other boys in my category were nowhere near to me in terms of physical build, and the fighters who could match me in height and weight were grown men. There was too much of a gulf in experience.

I would have to wait for three years.

During this time I was chomping at the bit, going mad with frustration, but I made sure to work on my game. Rather than sticking to the sparring partners at Jimmy Egan's club, Dad took me around the country so I could test myself against the pros. I battered them all over. My confidence was sky high and by the time I turned seventeen there were two other fighters in the country that were seemingly close to me in terms of physique – *finally*. One of them, a bloke called Duncan Lee, ended up knocking out the other competitor, so when a fight was arranged between the two of us, my first competitive bout ended up being a title decider for the position of the best junior super-heavyweight in the country.

But I couldn't have cared less about the accolades; nobody was going to stand in my way, least of all Duncan Lee, and I boxed his head off. After only one match, I was already a top-ranking boxer. As far as I was concerned, I'd barely started.

That's because amateur boxing wasn't the be all and end all for me. It was a rite of passage, something I had to go through, and I viewed my fights as preparation for the future, nothing more. In fact, the highlight of my amateur career was the day I finally turned pro. That said, there were some memorable moments during the journey. I represented both England, through the Steve Egan Boxing Academy, and Ireland, via the Smithboro Club in County Monaghan, and won thirty-one fights out of thirty-five. At that time, the soon-to-be Olympic fighter, David Price, was probably my biggest rival and he even defeated me in the 2006 north-west final of the ABA seniors, though he was several years older. Annoyingly, I never got to avenge the loss in the pro game, although it was something I was keen to do. In 2009, I even gave an interview to *Boxing Scene*, explaining how I wanted to punch Price's face in.

'When I fought him I was a raw, seventeen-year-old kid,' I said. 'He was twenty-three or something like that. I'd had ten bouts and he'd had seventy. He was a Commonwealth champion and had won all sorts while I was a novice. He was the only one who ended up on the floor and I was trying to catch him with big hooks while his style was totally suited to the amateurs. I was only a kid but I have come on so much since then . . . I'm a man now and he's definitely in my sights. If we fought again, Price wouldn't make it out of the first round. I'm too ferocious. He's just a big chinny thing from Liverpool.'

Not long afterwards, I got my first sniff of international recognition when it became apparent I was in the running for a place with Team GB for the 2008 Beijing Olympics. By that point I had won the ABA title, having defeated Damien Campbell 19–1 on points at York Hall, Bethnal Green. In the end, it turned out that my old adversary, David Price, had already been selected for the heavyweight place. For a while I tried to get to Beijing via the Irish team, but that route was eventually blocked off for political reasons.

I was nineteen years old. I would have turned twenty at the Games, which would have made for some party, but missing out proved to be an insignificance, mainly because of what I would go on to win during my pro career. (Of course, representing your country is a good thing. However, I wanted to be getting paid the big bucks for doing so, and it simply didn't happen at that level.) An Olympic medal wasn't exactly going to pay the bills or buy a nice house for Paris and myself. In my head, the fact that I had progressed from the club scene to the international stage – and been on the cusp of the Olympics – showed me I was on the right path. Winning all the gold medals wouldn't have made a blind bit of difference.

I also viewed the sport a little bit differently to the other lads in the England and Great Britain teams. We were travelling the world as kids, visiting places like Morocco, America, Serbia and Ukraine, which was a great experience.

But my teammates only ever talked about what they were going to do *after* their fights were done. They were forever chatting about going here and seeing that, whereas the only thing I looked forward to was the actual fight itself. It was the same when it came to winning the event, or getting into a medal position. I'd hear blokes saying things like, 'Well, if I get an easy draw there might be a chance of bronze.' But I didn't have any interest in that either. The match was all that mattered. Though I should have realised there was a gulf in attitudes when I saw some of the team hiding in the bushes during a training run one time, rather than working on their cardio.

There wasn't even a sense of pride within my family at the fact that I was representing our country. That's because everybody was busy doing their own thing and earning their own money, and very little changed when I turned pro. A TV interviewer recently asked me, 'Did everyone rally round and support you before a fight?' And the answer was: *No. Not really. They don't do it now when I am a world heavy-weight champion, and they didn't do it when I was a nobody.* Honestly, none of them gave a toss, even when a neighbour or somebody in the community started going on about how great it was that I'd represented my country, or succeeded at the top level. My family couldn't have cared if I was the world champion or a journeyman no-hoper; they couldn't have cared if I was a millionaire, or some bloke with only a tenner to his name. That's because they didn't get anything from me then, and they still don't now. They had their own lives and their own families to worry about. I respected them a million times more for behaving in that way rather than banging on about my successes, or sticking their hands out for money.

• • •

My first fight as a pro boxer came to me at the least convenient time: I was on my ten-day honeymoon with Paris in the Algarve, Portugal, when the offer landed from my new promoter, Mick Hennessy. I'd been invited to fight the Hungarian, Bela Gyongyosi at the Nottingham Arena on 6 December 2008 as the undercard of the Carl Froch v Jean Pascal super-middleweight championship fight. The contract arrived on the hotel fax machine.

Why the hell not? I thought. 'I agree. Let's do it.'

I was only two days into the holiday, but once the details had been passed over, I was flying home to train and prepare. I was about to become the best thing since sliced bread.

Paris was OK with my decision, and she'd known what was coming before the wedding. We had been together for around three years at that point, and throughout that time I'd travelled around a lot, fighting and training, and she had supported me every step of the way. For that, I owe her everything: if it hadn't been for Paris, 1) I probably wouldn't be alive right now, and 2) I never would have achieved my dreams. She helped me to stay grounded. Without her in my life, I'd have been out partying, clubbing and messing around with girls in my late teens and early twenties. Instead, I had a wife I loved dearly and a baby on the way – there's no way I could have run around like a lunatic. Those big life changes, aligned with my dedication to boxing, meant I was able to reach my full potential.

My turning pro felt inevitable to Paris; she knew there was no way I was staying an amateur boxer for long because I was already a wise head on young shoulders. One example: as a kid, still seventeen years old, I entered a competition called the ABA Senior Novice Championships. It was an event that any amateur boxer could enter providing they were under the age of thirty-five and had featured in no more than ten fights. I was beating men ten years older than me and in doing so I learned some big lessons about myself. The first: those fights were the very definition of man against boy, and yet I never felt intimidated. The second: my wins were never viewed as anything other than a functional event. Instead they were a sign of progression and every success was a stepping stone to much bigger things.

That mindset carried on throughout my career.

Even my first win as a professional against Gyongyosi

didn't feel like a big deal when it happened. It was shown live on ITV and packaged up in the usual glitz and glamour, but my thoughts after winning with a first round technical knockout were: *Yeah, great. But so what?* I wanted more and I wouldn't stop until I'd got it. I wanted to be the best. And I was determined to do everything in my power to get there.

But bloody hell, did I work hard to land that first pro paycheque. My routine was brutal and every day would follow the same timetable, where I ran for three or four miles in the morning and then trained for two hours at the boxing gym every night. I'd do bag work, barbell circuits, everything. I was the first into the gym and the last to leave, and I'd show up even when I wasn't supposed to. Mondays, Wednesdays and Fridays were for the proper boxers at the Jimmy Egan Boxing Academy, but I would train on the learner days as well, just to do my own thing. On weekends, I'd wander in with Shane for even more work. I was non-stop.

If there was one flaw in my game, it was my nutrition; I ate whatever I wanted, whenever I wanted it. Sometimes I'd finish a session in the gym and head straight to the fish and chip shop. I wouldn't think twice about wolfing down a bag of sweets, or eating a couple of pies during the day. I was a heavyweight boxer. I didn't have to worry about being under a certain weight; *I had to be over one.* And besides, it wasn't affecting my march towards the big leagues, so why did I have to stress? I was young. I could run a sausage roll and chips off in no time at all.

• • •

Life changed once I'd turned pro and in so many ways. All my fights seemed to be on the telly, which meant more and more people were recognising me in the street. My rising stardom was furthered as I came to understand the value of being an entertainer, which was something I'd learned from the boxing greats, like Muhammad Ali, Prince Naseem and Mike Tyson. I understood that my reputation could be furthered by simply making the right comment and at the right time. So in my first-ever press conference I took a swipe at the reigning heavyweight champion, Wladimir Klitschko, by claiming I was a better fighter than him and with superior movement to boot. 'I will beat him one day,' I said. The journalists lapped it up. During my youth, I'd flogged cars; now I was selling myself, and within a year I was super famous. My televised fights drew audiences of millions.

Everywhere I went, people wanted photos and autographs, but fame never affected me. It felt normal, like an everyday event, because in a way it was. As an amateur, people spoke about me in the media, they told me I was going to win the lot, so the attention I received having turned pro wasn't exactly out of the blue. It didn't turn my head either. I suppose it was a bit like being a car dealer who trades in Rolls-Royces, Bentleys and Porsches: if that same dealer walks past one of those motors in the street, they won't bat an eyelid. I was the same when people wanted me to sign a piece of paper or pose for a selfie. *Just another day, Tyson, my boy.*

As for the money side, I was paid nine grand for my pro debut, but I didn't celebrate by purchasing anything flashy because I already had everything I needed – a career in boxing; a new wife who was pregnant; and a 2008 Mercedes E-Class. When I'd travelled to Nottingham for the fight against Gyongyosi, I wore a Rolex watch. Once in the venue I overheard the American promoter, Gary Shaw, nudge someone alongside him.

'Who is that guy?' he said.

That's Tyson Fury, a new heavyweight.

'A new heavyweight?' he said. 'This guy don't need boxing. He's got the same watch as me!'

When I was eventually paid, my first job was to go to the bank and deposit the cheque. Then I left it alone. I didn't touch the money for ages because Dad had taught me not to waste my earnings on crap. He said, 'If you get any money, invest it in bricks and mortar. It's a slow return but it'll pay off in the end . . .' He was right too. By the age of twenty-one I'd paid off my mortgage, but I'd also earned enough to buy a gunmetal grey Range Rover Sport, the same one James Bond drives in the movie, *Skyfall*. Really, I couldn't have done any better. I was rolling deep with a big grin on my face, knowing that I was going to prove all the doubters wrong. If anyone had questioned my chances of making it after watching my appearance on *The Gloves Are Off*, they had overlooked one simple truth. I might have had the money already, but I also possessed a secret weapon: the heart of a champion.

CHAPTER TWELVE

TO THE MOON

My first year or three as a pro set a blistering pace. To anyone paying attention I was a young man on the move, with no real desire to slow down for anything, or anyone, as I smashed my goals and tenderised my opponents like slabs of meat. If one slogan encapsulated this thrilling period, it was the line made famous by Buzz Lightyear, the *Toy Story* hero who famously shouted, *'To infinity . . . and beyond!'* That's because I was being launched on a rocket ride to the stars and anyone hoping to join me had to strap in tight.

Don't believe me? Well, check the stats.

2008: one fight, one win.

2009: eight fights, eight wins.

2010: four fights, four wins.

I was racking up the victories like nobody's business.

There were standout battles along the way. After Bela Gyongyosi I faced Marcel Zeller, a German fighter nick-named The Highlander, on 17 January 2009. *Was this a risky choice?* Maybe. Zeller was only my second-ever professional fight; the bloke had twenty knockouts to his name and I shouldn't have been taking him on at that early stage. But I wasn't fazed, as proven by a technical knockout in the third.

A couple of months later, I fought Lee Swaby, a former kickboxer, in a six-rounder at the Aston Events Centre, Birmingham. The match was shown on ITV's *Fight Night* and Swaby was considered an experienced and potentially tricky adversary, what with his twenty-three wins, twenty-two losses and two draws over a twelve-year career. No bother. I smacked him about over the first four rounds and he retired in his corner. In fact, the closest he came to hurting me was in the final minute or so when I unloaded a massive uppercut on his chin, missed, and smacked myself in the face. *Not my finest moment.*

The other highlight during this time was Scott 'Ding Ding' Belshaw in May 2009. Belshaw was a 6 foot 7, Northern Irish fighter with ten wins and one defeat and was a genuine boss – he was tipped to be a big deal for the future. Belshaw was also close to me in size, so the expectation was for a really tight contest. While I hated to be a buzzkill, the bloke just wasn't at my level. I rocked up and took Belshaw quickly, bloodying his nose and knocking him down twice in the first. When I smacked him hard in the guts in the second, the ref ended the fight. I'd hurt him so badly with that one punch that I held back on my next. It felt like the right thing to do, even though it would have been a clean headshot.

'That was good sportsmanship by Fury,' said the ITV co-commentator, Duke McKenzie afterwards. 'He could have continued the combination, continued throwing the punches, [he] looked at his opponent, saw that he was hurt and stopped the onslaught . . .'

Although I was determined to be the world champion, I never took the sport too seriously, which would become a pattern throughout my entire career. Yeah, I loved boxing. I was passionate and determined, focused on beating up everyone in my path, but the contests were fun and I felt very relaxed about the pressures associated with them. In that respect I was probably unique. Whenever I noticed other promising fighters coming through the ranks – some of them with the talent to make it to the very top – they seemed stressed about every aspect of their game. It was as if they were trying to hold on to a wet bar of soap. Gripping too tightly was causing it to pop from their fingers.

I was the opposite. Before matches, the other boxer was viewed as a bloke I had to beat, nothing more, and no opponent was placed on a pedestal, regardless of what they might have achieved in the past. The downside to my laid-back attitude was that in between fights, if there wasn't a challenger in the diary I couldn't see any point in training, or maintaining my fighting weight, so I went out all the time. Meanwhile, I was still eating all the wrong foods and it was starting to show. One minute the scales showed 17 stone; a month of pies and pints later and I was pushing past 20 stone.

Because I was getting fatter and fatter, the training became harder and harder. The more weight I put on, the more I had to burn off, but my problems were down to mindset. When I had a target in sight, I stuck to my training schedule ferociously. But I found it very difficult to focus when there wasn't an event to prepare for. This flaw in my preparation was really only sorted once I moved into my second career. Luckily, it didn't seem to affect my knockout power too badly.

● ● ●

I loved the turnover of fights throughout 2009 because as a young boxer it was good to be active all the time. I wanted to be in the thick of it; I wanted to be earning money; I wanted to be learning and showcasing my skills. I also knew that by not being active I ran the risk of slipping off the radar. A lot of emerging boxers went AWOL simply by not fighting enough, and when that happened the fans tended to lose interest in their progress. With nobody paying any attention, those guys eventually left the sport for another life. Not me, I kept myself busy and before long my biggest fight to date was being arranged for September, 2009: a ten-round clash with John McDermott in an English heavyweight title match at the Brentwood Centre, Essex.

McDermott was eight years older than me and came

in at around 6 foot 3, so I was going to tower over him in the ring. But he was a good fighter, the reigning champion, having defeated Pelé Reid in 2008, and would eventually become a three-time challenger for the British title (without winning it). Though McDermott would reclaim his English title in 2013, his main flaw was a lack of power. That said, he was still a step up from the calibre of boxer I'd been used to facing and the fans wondered if I was getting ahead of myself, as they had done with Zeller, Swaby and Belshaw. I wasn't worried about him though. In the build-up I gave him a series of nicknames – McMuffin, McDoughnut and the Big Mac. I don't think he liked it very much.

The first nine rounds of the bout were a bruising grind but I hung in there, biding my time, taking shots whenever I could. Then McDermott hit me with a solid right-hander. I felt it. My head wobbled, my body stiffened, but I managed to stay strong and cuffed him about the head a few times. In these moments, it's important that a fighter shows courage. I certainly wasn't going to back down because in my head I was battling for my family and my name – *for everything* – and McDermott was going to have to knock me out to win.

Weirdly, that isn't the attitude in all boxers. When a fight goes horribly wrong, some blokes will try anything to get out the ring without losing face, rather than taking their medicine. I have even heard of fighters biting their opponents or throwing a series of low blows in an attempt to get kicked out. But that is only another form of cowardice because they are really just angling for a referee to show them the door. That way they can say, 'Oh, I was thrown out for some nonsense . . .' In their heads, disqualification is more respectable than getting battered, or throwing in the towel.

That wasn't going to wash with me. I would do anything in my power to leave a fight victorious, though I wouldn't stoop so low as to clump someone in the bollocks, or anything daft. If I ended up losing, well I was big enough to accept the result and say, 'Fantastic fight, mate. Well done.'

Against John McDermott I had to bite down on my gumshield to stay in what was a physically punishing bout, but in the end it was my hand the ref was lifting, not McDermott's. After ten rounds, I'd won on points, while showing the world that I had a solid chin and plenty of stamina, but my opponent's camp were clearly unhappy about the decision. They called it a disgrace, and they're entitled to their opinions of course. It certainly wasn't a good performance from me – a two out of ten probably – but I showed enough grit and determination to pull through, so I was happy.

'If he wants a rematch, let's get it on,' I said afterwards. 'I'll stop him next time. It was an off night, but I still got the better of him . . .'

During this busy part of my life, I hadn't yet made the

connection between the time I spent eating well and train-ing hard and my mental wellbeing. (Reminder: the more I work, the happier I feel; when I don't train, I feel like rubbish.) Sadly, 2009 was a one-off and my schedule changed dramatically as I advanced through the boxing ranks. I was learning that the more successful a fighter becomes, the more he has to put himself into title fights. And while that is undoubtedly a good thing, those bouts take a long time to organise because a promoter needs months to arrange the contracts and sell tickets. That meant the number of con-tests on my schedule were reduced. Once I'd won the Eng-lish heavyweight championship, I found myself facing fewer and fewer opponents, which gave me more time to drift.

During 2010, I was involved in four matches, defeating Hans-Joerg Blasko, John McDermott (again), Rich Power (a name nearly as impressive as mine) and Zack Page. But really, everything was gearing towards an eventual, inevit-able showdown with the Ukrainian powerhouse, Wladimir 'Dr Steelhammer' Klitschko – the reigning IBF, WBO and IBO heavyweight title-holder. I wanted to knock him out more than anything in the world, but my obsession wasn't about winning the belts – though that was an undeniably brilliant bonus. It was about beating the man. If I could pummel a boxer of Klitschko's reputation, legend status would arrive overnight. It was a moment I would dream about for the next five years.

My motivation was clear: Klitschko was a big name having first won the WBO title in 2000 at the age of twenty-four. By the time I arrived on the scene in 2008, he'd lost his belt and reclaimed it again, but it was my opinion that his successes were down to the professional team that operated around him. From what I could tell, they acted more like a business than a boxing crew. Meanwhile Klitschko and his people were supreme athletes and educated to the hilt (the man himself had a PhD in sports science). That was very different to how I operated. Given my advantage in size and speed, I could take him, and he knew it too.

That understanding had come about because in 2010 we had the chance to study each other up close when his trainer, Manny Steward, asked me to travel to Austria to work from his camp, where he was training Klitschko. Being in the same space, at the same time, was an eye-opening experience.

This bloke isn't invincible! I thought. *He's just a lad in a pair of boxing gloves doing what I do every single day.*

Previously, I'd thought of him as an Ivan Drago character, the Russian villain from *Rocky IV*, but I'd allowed myself to become distracted by the glitz and glamour that surrounded a world champion. I'd gone against my own rule: I'd put him on a pedestal. In reality, Klitschko was just another bare bum in the shower. Getting up close allowed me to see past the myth.

To work my way towards the top dog, I had to beat Derek Chisora, a vicious, 27-year-old British boxer with an identical 14–0 record to me. Chisora was then the British and Commonwealth heavyweight champion and the WBO's Number Twelve ranked fighter. His hope at the time was also to fight Klitschko for the world title and a date had been set for the end of 2010, but it was postponed when the Ukrainian tore an abdominal muscle in training. Suddenly I was the next name on Chisora's list as a challenger for his British title, but rumours soon circulated that he was OK with vacating the belt. I would have to fight someone else for it, which really didn't work for me. I was twenty-two at the time and keen to defeat the champion, the face that everyone knew. I always believed you should take a title off the holder; you didn't fish it out of a bin.

The chance to put my point across arrived at a sold-out O2 Arena in London during the fight between James DeGale and George Groves in May 2011. Having taken a seat, my Uncle Hughie pointed to Chisora in the crowd. *Jackpot.* I hadn't gone there to watch the boxing; I was really only interested in calling him out. I always demanded first choice and Chisora was the bloke I wanted to fight next. I was also impatient, in a now-or-never type of mood, which probably explains the events that followed.

Right, I thought, standing up. 'I've had enough of this.'

The WBO inter-continental welterweight title between Frankie Gavin and Young Mutley was taking place on the undercard, but I could not have given a monkeys. I ran to where I knew Chisora was sitting and worked my way past security.

When I saw him in his seat, I started yelling. 'Oi, Chisora!'

There was no response, so I shouted again. 'Del Boy! Oi!'

When Chisora eventually turned around, he looked shocked to see me. 'Who do you think you are, talking about me in the papers?,' I said. 'I'm going to knock you out when you eventually get in the ring.'

Chisora then responded by claiming there hadn't been enough money on offer for the match.

'I fight for honour, not money, mate,' I shouted, tearing my shirt off. 'I'll fight you here and now, pal!'

It was all a show, I just wanted him to sign the deal, but to anyone watching, it probably looked as if I'd lost my mind, especially Chisora. He was terrified and unsure of how to handle the escalating situation. The same went for Frank Warren, his promoter at the time. He had been sitting nearby. 'Go away!' he shouted.

'Screw you, you old sausage,' I yelled back. 'You can have it too. Send that shithouse to me right now.'

A team of bouncers edged towards me. I spotted them in my peripheral vision. 'First one that comes close enough, I'm chinning,' I said.

Knowing I'd outstayed my welcome, I exited the building surrounded by a 25-strong mob of security guards. I paid £100 for my ticket and yet I didn't get to see more than a few minutes of boxing. Cheekily, I asked for a refund, even though there was no chance of getting one, but I could not have cared less. The scene had worked. Within a day or so, a July date for the British heavyweight title decider was set and our meeting was nicknamed *The Big Brawl: To Settle It All.* Shortly afterwards the two of us were sitting down together at a press conference, with me explaining to the world how I was going to smash Chisora into next week.

At that time, Chisora was the clear favourite; most people had him down to batter me inside three rounds and I was hearing the same old story, as always: *Fury's taking on too much of a risk!* Or, *He's out of his depth – it's too fast too soon!* In fact, one of the few people backing me to win was Manny Steward. In an interview, he said, 'Tyson's sheer physical size; he's got a good chin, good stamina, and good punch output, also. I think those factors, and being at 6 foot 9 compared to 6 foot 1 is going to be a big problem for Derek to overcome. I may be a little crazy, but I give a slight edge to Tyson in this fight.' We both knew my punch was too much for Chisora. The plan was to hit him in the face as hard and as fast as I could because he wouldn't be able to live with it.

I also had extra incentive because Klitschko was claiming that he would consider fighting the eventual winner. That kind of talk went on all the time in boxing, without actually going anywhere – there were plenty of obstacles to hurdle when organising a world title contest. But all of a sudden, a shot at the heavyweight world champion seemed more in play than ever. Sure, winning the British and Commonwealth heavyweight belts would be nice, but getting to smash Klitschko as a reward was what I was all about.

Earning that chance by dispatching Chisora turned out not to be too much of a problem. Nearly 3 million people tuned in to Channel 5 as I jabbed his ears off over twelve rounds, winning on a unanimous decision. I was twenty-two years old. Finally the world was coming to understand that I was destined for greatness. Maybe Klitschko had seen it too, because his promise to give the winner a world title chance seemed to evaporate. It wouldn't materialise for another four years. Why that was, I'm not exactly sure, but Klitschko was a control freak. When he couldn't handle an opponent, I think he got scared. The thought of facing a 6 foot 9, Gypsy wild man who did what he wanted, fought how he wanted and said what he wanted, probably didn't appeal to him.

Meanwhile, I was licking my lips at the idea of taking him down. I was happy to wait patiently too, trusting that everything was happening for a reason.

'When my time comes, I'll be the world champion,' I thought.

Little did I know that achieving my dreams would twist into a nightmare.

CHAPTER THIRTEEN

I HATE MYSELF AND
I WANT TO DIE

There's a saying that goes, 'Hard times make tough men . . .' and I was working my dick off, so I must have been as strong as anything. It soon became clear that to get to Wladimir Klitschko I would have to beat the toughest and hungriest contenders in the heavyweight division and my journey began in 2011 when I packed off Nicolai Firtha of the USA. Next up was the Bosnian-born Canadian, Nevan Pajkić, as I retained my Commonwealth heavyweight title. Then in 2012, I cleaned out the Americans Vinny Maddalone and Kevin Johnson. The WBC title had become vacant following the retirement of Vitali Klitschko and I was hopeful that, because of my results, I would be lined up to fight Bermane Stiverne for the belt. Instead, the powers-that-be placed Stiverne and Chris Arreola in the title match, even though they'd fought just a year previously.

No bother, I cracked on, and in April, 2013 I fought Steve Cunningham in Madison Square Garden: *New York City, baby*. This was my US debut and for running the risk of having my head knocked off on TV I was offered just ten grand, which was barely enough to cover my training camp and team travel. 'Whatever,' I thought, 'I'll take it.' I knew that at some point I wanted to break America, like the Beatles, the Stones, and all those other British bands over the years, and a televised fight in the States would make for a good start. I was also unable to get Klitschko to fight me at that point, so what else was I going to do, sit around scratching my bollocks all day? Instead, I rocked up to the MSG determined to make an impression, giving Cunningham some mouth as I danced around in the opening round.

'Come on,' I shouted, laughing at him. 'That ain't nothing.' I even shoved him after the first was over.

Then I let my guard down. Cunningham knocked me over with a sweeping, overhand right in the second, and while it was a warning sign, it didn't deter me from playing the showman. I jabbed at my own head and raised my arms in an attempt to bring him on as I skipped across the canvas. By the seventh I'd absorbed everything Cunningham could throw at me, wearing him down with some big hits. A body shot sent him to the ropes and as he wobbled, I clumped him with a right to the head. I think it might have sent him into Pennsylvania.

With every fight, I got a little closer to Klitschko, but I would need to fight three more times before laying a glove on him. The first was against the American Joey Abell in February 2014, who I took in the fourth round despite not being on top form. I then stopped Derek Chisora in the tenth at the ExCel Centre in London in our second fight the following November. I then faced the Romanian-German Christian Hammer in a WBO title final eliminator – the fight took place in February 2015 at the O2 Arena and I sent him packing in eight rounds. Klitschko could run away from me no longer – the only thing left for him to settle was a time and a place.

Despite these victories, it was a dark time. That same year, Uncle Hughie, who had trained me for the first part of my career, was in hospital having been hurt in an accident. While moving a caravan, he'd snapped his leg when a drawbar fell on him, and though that might not sound like a life-threatening injury, the blow created a blood clot. It moved around his body and into his lungs, and he eventually suffered a heart attack.

Hughie, who I loved dearly, was placed in an induced coma. For nearly three months I visited him in Wythenshawe Hospital in Manchester. At one point, Paris was on another ward in the same building, having experienced a miscarriage, and for a little while I bounced between the two beds. It was a horrible time, no one's ever really prepared for traumatic news like the passing of a baby, not fully. Hughie would eventually pass away from his injuries.

Losing him was a real blow because the pair of us been close. As my first-ever pro trainer, Hughie coached me to a 17–0 record and a position in the world's top ten. Weirdly, it wasn't just about how good a trainer he was. Our success partly came about because we were both living on the same site as the gym. And when I say 'gym', I really mean a glorified shed where the temperatures were boiling in the summer and freezing cold in the winter. (And when it rained, water pissed in through the roof.) I didn't give a crap though. Discomfort was an emotional state I thrived in, and other than training there wasn't anything else I wanted to do. I suppose if your every waking minute is dedicated to one thing, you're going to get pretty good at it. That's if you have the skill to back it up.

Hughie and me worked twice a day, nearly every day, with a set routine: running in the mornings; weights and boxing in the afternoons. I loved every second of it and learned a lot, even though he had no real background in being a pro boxing coach, other than the fact that he'd trained two other fighters – his son was one, the other was a journeyman. Hughie had boxed himself, but as with a lot of people I would come to work with during my career, he had no real resume to speak of. That's because he didn't need one. When you've got the fastest horse on the track you don't need to be the greatest trainer in the world. If that beast was so much quicker than everyone else in the field it was going to win regardless.

I still learned a lot under Uncle Hughie. As I sparred,

I often heard him shouting instructions at me. His words came at me like mantras.

Do damage with every punch.

Keep it long. Keep it moving . . .

. . . Keep moving. Keep angling.

He instinctively knew what I was good at and though he might not have had a hundred world-class fighters on his CV, or years and years of coaching experience, that didn't mean he wasn't good at what he did. He taught me how to turn my knuckles over when I threw a punch and helped to transform me from an amateur boxer into a seasoned pro. During a fight, Uncle Hughie was also very calm. He delivered clear instructions from the corner and knew how I could beat an opponent, usually with one look. In a split second he'd assess the other guy's weak spots before formulating a game plan to take him down. Whenever I went back to my corner after a bad round, Uncle Hughie's advice always got me back on track.

Together we had a lot of great times in the gym. I was going to miss him badly.

The loss of my baby was devastating too. I postponed one fight so Paris and I could come to terms with what had happened, but really I was bottling everything up because I wanted to stay strong for my showdown with Klitschko. In many ways, the thought of fighting him had been keeping my dark emotions in check for years, but the issues were only being compartmentalised, like odd socks being shoved in a drawer — I was depressed, anxious and frazzled with OCD. My mental health was a mess and the goal of unseating the reigning world champion, while giving me focus, was nothing more than a distraction from the truth. I was an emotional time bomb and the clock was ticking.

I didn't have room to mourn; I didn't have room to deal with all the problems that were mounting up. I was on a psychological rollercoaster and in 2015 I piled on the weight, at one point hitting 25 stone. My love for boxing was fading too. After a date had been announced for the Klitschko fight on 24 October, I shrugged. 'Who gives a toss?' I thought. I was emotionally broken, all over the place, despite the fact I was finally getting my opportunity to face the world champion, a man I'd spent the last seven years hoping to beat.

● ● ●

One other adversary I was supposed to take on during that time was David Haye.

But he didn't fight me because he was a shithouse. I'm not saying any more about him in my book. He's really not worth the ink.

● ● ●

Beating Wladimir Klitschko was probably my most spectacular moment in the ring, because firstly, it showed the world what I was truly capable of and secondly, it was so utterly against the odds that not many people could believe it had actually happened. That night, everyone's attitude about me changed. When you finish a living legend in any sport, it sets a benchmark, but the fight in the Esprit Arena in Düsseldorf was a gladiatorial masterclass and a pugilistic portrait; an absolute peach in every department. Over twelve rounds I hammered the guy's head to bits using the sweet, sweet science of boxing, nullifying him so he couldn't unload his big right hand. Sure, he'd been knocked over by fighters in his career – if you have enough bouts you're bound to walk into a big punch from time to time – but he'd never been given a lesson like the one he received in Germany. Klitschko got the fight of his life.

I traced the victory back to our very first press conference, where I'd dressed as Batman (more on that later). It got into Klitschko's head. Later, I confused him by claiming that I couldn't have cared less about reigning as a champ or building a legacy. Instead I was fixated on beating him.

'Oh, wouldn't you like all my belts?' he said.

I shook my head. 'Nope, you keep them things. All I want to do is break your face in, that's it. I'm not interested in your belts or your fame or your glory, I just want to beat you up in a fight.'

Everybody thought I was messing about, but I wasn't.

With all the antics, mucking around, and name-calling that followed, I showed Klitschko a level of disrespect that he wasn't used to. It was unsettling for him and he didn't seem to have a strategy for neutralising my behaviour, though fair play, he had a go. In the run-up to the contest, there were a few stunts here and there, but everything was telegraphed and destined to backfire.

The fun and games started at the weigh-in. When Klitschko showed up, I did a double take.

'Is he wearing platform boots, or has he been eating all his greens?' I thought. 'Because he looks taller than me.'

According to the stats he was supposed to be three inches shorter.

Later, when I stepped on the scales, all sorts of weirdness happened. The officials seemed to think that an eleven-year-old version of Tyson Fury had arrived for the occasion, because a number flashed up (17 stone 9 pounds) I'd not seen for over fifteen years. (I had lost around six stone in the build-up to the fight by drinking only one protein drink a day and was around 19 stone, but the number that day was a lot lighter.) My uncle Peter, who was training me at the time, looked confused. He wanted to know what I had, or hadn't been eating.

'They're cheating,' I told him. 'They're trying to get inside my head. But it's not going to work . . .'

Things got worse on the day of the fight, when I visited the venue to check out the ring. As I walked across the surface, my legs were light, like I was about to be sprung into the air. The canvas felt as if it had been stuffed with memory foam and moving across it was like bouncing over a trampoline. Given my quick feet and agility, I knew the ring had been designed that way to knacker me out, a fact that was confirmed when the former world cruiserweight champion and Sky Sports commentator, Johnny Nelson, told me that Klitschko had been training with an identical canvas in his camp.

'Right, I'm not having this,' I said. 'I don't care about the money or the titles, I only want to beat the man . . . But if he's not fighting fair we'll go home.'

Arguments raged throughout the day. With only an hour to go, the canvas was swapped, but rows were kicking off all over the place and a lot of them had to do with the gloves. As the mandatory challenger in a world title fight, I was entitled to a set of my choosing. I'd ordered a pair of puncher's gloves, but what arrived felt more like a pair of duck feather pillows.

Don't care, I thought. *I'll still give him a bruising with these.*

As my hands were wrapped in the dressing room, Klitschko's brother, Vitali hovered about me, watching the process like a hawk, as he was entitled to do. This was a procedure that took place before every championship fight and a way of ensuring no funny business went on. But when my dad walked to Klitschko's dressing room to make the same checks, Dr Steelhammer's fists were already bandaged. His gloves were on and he was ready to go.

'You can take them off and do it all again,' said Dad. 'Don't think we won't sod off home.'

My thinking was that Klitschko could have attempted these mind games with his previous challengers. (Though I'm not sure.) But I wasn't backing down. This was my moment in history. I was a one-man army on a mission, and convinced that nobody would get between my destiny and me that night. Weirdly, it seemed as if Klitschko had arrived at the exact same opinion. During the walk-in, he looked scared. We hadn't even exchanged bombs and he seemed beaten. Meanwhile, the expression on my face was spinning a very different story.

It said: Am I bothered by you? *No.*

Am I scared of you? *No.*

Do I give a crap about what you can do? *No, because I'm going to batter you to bits.*

From the first round, my plan was to swoop away from Klitschko's biggest shots, all while changing from the ortho-dox to southpaw stance. When the opportunity arrived I wanted to pop off some killer jabs that softened him for the bigger hits. That, I reckoned, was my best chance of keeping him on his toes. The bloke had a huge punch and he carried a vicious streak, but my natural movement and quick feet were probably enough to avoid a lot of what he had.

When my longer reach and pillow-like gloves connected with Klitschko's skull for the first time, it set a routine. I rocked him over and over during a twelve-round siege that wore him down to dust. My concentration became laser-sighted; I wasn't flinching, or showboating. I didn't even attempt to wind him up as we grappled. Forget whispering poisoned nothings into his ear, or goading him with arm gestures and funny faces, I was finishing Klitschko's reign with clinical, tactical precision.

My corner was yelling instructions. They ordered me to go forward. I heard voices telling me to switch it up, to change my approach, but the game plan was unsettling Klitschko. I saw it in his face, so I kept on going. Combination after combination landed hard; by the fight's midpoint a cut had cracked open under his right eye. In the end, the last few rounds moved like one-way traffic: I hit. Klitschko suffered. And I out-boxed him so comprehensively that his trainer, Johnathon Banks, reportedly delivered a worrying message in his corner before the tenth began. *The only way you're going to beat Fury is by knocking him out.* But there was no way he was knocking me out – I just wouldn't allow it.

When the bell clanged for the end of the twelfth, I knew I'd won, and he knew it too. Klitschko had never fought anyone like me before. But how could he? I was a one-off,

incomparable to any other fighter, and impossible to prepare for because I fought southpaw and orthodox; I could
be a puncher or a hitter; I was a motherfucking bamboozler,
and unlike anyone he had fought in the past few years.

As my victory was made official, the IBF, WBO, WBA
(Super), IBO and *The Ring* heavyweight championship of
the world changed hands. (Deontay Wilder held the WBC
title at that time, by the way.) Tears streamed down my
face, I had worked so hard for my shot all while enduring
a seemingly endless payload of physical and mental suffering. But having beaten Klitschko I was also monumentally
screwed: the world was at my feet and all my dreams had
been fulfilled. So what else was there to live for?

Nothing.

And that made me a dead man walking.

• • •

A couple of years ago I went into a recording studio with
the pop legend, Robbie Williams. The plan was to record
a song for his Christmas album and I had a great time
doing it because Robbie's a top bloke and we had plenty
in common, especially when it came to the subject of
mental health. Robbie and me are both people that have
hit the top, having worked hard for something all our
lives – him: pop stardom; me: the world heavyweight

championship — only for the realities of our success to become massively destructive and very different to what we'd expected at the beginning.

Robbie referred to this feeling as Paradise Syndrome, describing it as situation that forced a person to ask serious questions of themselves: *Is this really what I worked for? Is this everything from now on?* Having achieved the impossible, a person with Paradise Syndrome feels empty without a new target to aim at, or some fresh cause to work for. It's why a lot of astronauts have struggled emotionally after returning from space. When a person sets foot on the moon, or performs a spacewalk, it must be hard to know what to do for an encore. I reckon it's the same for people that dream of winning the National Lottery. When it happens, the buzz is great, but short-lived, and the aftermath can be traumatic. Let me tell you right now: if a cheque with *all* the money arrived on your doorstep, the unexpected wealth would probably destroy your life quite quickly.

Having reflected on this time in my life, this was exactly the position I found myself in having defeated Klitschko and winning nearly every title going. In many ways I had won the lottery, except my success was earned through hard work rather than luck, and up until that point, I believed it was what I truly wanted. At the beginning of my first career — from my amateur days to 28 November 2015 — the aim had been to defeat the reigning champion.

Once I'd got there, I had achievements to my name, I had glory, money, and everything that a person could want from life, but I realised very quickly that it wasn't the be-all and end-all of everything. Coming to that understanding was a psychologically crushing blow and all the issues I'd been suppressing over the past few years – my mental health, Paris's miscarriage, Uncle Hughie's death – rose to the surface at once.

In many ways, I knew the pain was coming because I knew I was going to win and that a victory would leave me with nothing to aim for. That caused me to become increasingly depressed during the build-up to the fight as I realised my life was going to be over afterwards. Beating Klitschko had been my purpose, to the point where it was an almost unhealthy obsession, and if you took a person's purpose away, there was no point in them hanging around anymore. I think it's why some people really struggle once they retire – without a goal or cause they're just waiting to die and their body and mind slowly start to fail afterwards. I was facing a similar situation.

As I sparred one day in the training camp, I remember one of my partners asking me what I was going to do once Klitschko was beaten.

My response was shocking. 'I'll tell you what I'm going to do: I'm going to be depressed for about three years, and I'll probably never box again.'

I can't remember exactly how the other bloke responded, whether he laughed or took the piss, but I know he didn't believe me. Worryingly, I was being honest. I sensed a dark cloud was about to shadow my life and there was nowt I could do to stop it. That's because I didn't understand what was happening to me. Depression was an enemy that swung its bombs from the shadows and I hadn't been trained to duck and weave away from the pain.

Everything came crashing down in the minutes after the fight. By the time I'd walked to the press conference, I was at an all-time low. My mood was just as bleak the following morning, even though I was the newly crowned, unified heavyweight champion of the world. Having woken up at the hotel and wandered downstairs, I bumped into a few members of my team.

One of them said, 'You're going to have a lovely career now, Tyson.'

I just couldn't see it. 'Nope, I'm never going to box again. Probably never see any of you lot again, either . . .'

Like my comments in the training camp, nobody took my attitude seriously. They thought I was messing around. As far as they were concerned, I was going to be the happiest man in the world.

An avalanche of misery hit me from the minute I returned to Britain. Hindsight's always clear as day, but at the time I had no idea that the family tragedies I'd experienced hadn't been acknowledged in a healthy way. Shutting them out and focusing on Klitschko was the wrong move, and suddenly, with no target to concentrate on, the gathering pain of losing my baby boy to a miscarriage rushed in. It wasn't the first child we had lost in that way either. Paris suffered three miscarriages, and the grief for all of them overwhelmed me at once. At the same time I was struck by the new void in my life: Uncle Hughie was gone; I wouldn't see him at the house or in the gym anymore. I was rocked. In many ways, we don't really ever process death in a rational way. It's as if we don't really believe the person has gone. That has been my experience anyway.

Meanwhile, I was riding the hurricane of becoming the nation's favourite pantomime villain, the bloke everybody loved to hate. As I explained in *Behind The Mask*, I had previously believed that it was important for a fighter to cultivate a notorious reputation in the early days of their career because it created a buzz before fights. But my antics were a front, a facade, something I put on whenever I wanted to grab the limelight. I'd clearly gone too far and lost my grip on what was the real me, and what was an actor playing a role.

I also felt as if some of my achievements were being undervalued, or dismissed. But the bottom line was that I was the heavyweight champion of the world. Surely I deserved to be recognised for that?

My reaction: 'If this is what success is about, you can take it and get stuffed with it. I've hit all my targets, and now I don't even want to live anymore.'

The time to push my self-destruct button had arrived.

• • •

Every day was horrendous. I didn't want to do anything, because boxing meant nothing to me, even though a rematch with Klitschko was being organised. Instead, I got up when I wanted, ate what I wanted and drank as much as I wanted. As for the training? Stick that. I couldn't see the point, not when dossing about the house and eating junk food felt like the right thing to do. When I did go into the gym, I stood back and willed on my sparring partners. I wanted them to unload on me and wouldn't defend myself because I was in self-harm mode – I needed to be punished. The hours seemed to shoot by me like bullets and before long they became days, weeks and months – 2015 blurred into 2016 and I couldn't tell either of them apart. As I slid towards rock bottom, the experience of simply existing felt like pissing in the wind.

My daily routine collapsed at the end of 2015 and into 2016, and I piled on a ton of weight, shooting up to 30 stone. That only added to the sensations of listlessness and self-loathing. Whenever I looked in the mirror, I stared into the eyes of somebody I hated. He was a big, fat pig and a useless dosser. A man with everything who wanted to chuck it away. He didn't know where he was going or what to do next. He was a shadow of his former glory. He deserved death. Most of all he was a mentally unstable person who didn't know how to ask for help.

Paris and the kids suffered a lot during this time because my mood swings were up and down, and round and round. One minute I was happy and ready to make things right, the next I was sad, though, really, I had been like that for as long as I could remember. It wasn't unheard of for me to change my mind on something thirty times in a day. One minute I was deadly serious about an idea – like going away for a weekend, for example, or learning to play the piano – the next I lost interest. I made rash decisions very quickly. This game of emotional Swingball only intensified during the height of my illness.

Everything was lost. I really didn't see the point in going on and I was as emotionally low as any person could be without actually dying. When I woke up some mornings, my first thought would be one of desolation. *Why did I wake up today? Why didn't I die in my sleep?* Depression and mental illness had their hands around my throat and the grip was slowly squeezing the life from me. Everything felt dark and empty. So I tried to drink it away.

A lot of the time I went to the pub with my brothers,

even though the house was being renovated during 2016 and Paris, the kids and me were living in a caravan. Rather than looking after the family I turned my back on all responsibilities and got drunk because booze helped to silence my depression for a few merciful hours. I downed anywhere between ten and eighteen pints in a sitting and sometimes the required change took place: the one in which the inner voices telling me that I was worthless were silenced and the old Tyson Fury came roaring back. What I didn't know then, like so many other things regarding mental health, was that you couldn't drink the illness away. Those moments were nothing more than a sticking plaster on a gaping wound and once the hangover had kicked in the following day, I was back to square one.

I went on benders for days and Paris would understandably fear the worst. The kids were just as confused; they didn't know what was happening to Daddy. The thing is, even though I was going against my morals by drinking heavily and turning my back on the family, I didn't give a flying hoot at the time, because shame and embarrassment doesn't have any impact when you're mentally unwell and wanting to die. They're the emotions of a sane person and I definitely wasn't that. Thank God Paris stood by me.

While all of this was kicking off, in the weeks after the fight, the IBF stripped me of the heavyweight belt. As the holder I was obliged to fight their mandatory challenger, the 31-year-old Ukrainian, Vyacheslav Glazkov, who had won twenty-one of his twenty-two pro fights. But I'd already signed a rematch clause with Klitschko and there was no way of doing both. On this occasion the belt was taken away because I wouldn't face Glazkov. It all felt a bit unfair. As far as I was concerned the IBF were dead to me. I'd have rather pissed on their belt than fight for it again.

And yet, the worst of my meltdown hadn't shown itself, but it was coming. I could feel it. Like that shaken-up bottle of fizzy pop I mentioned earlier, the time to explode had arrived.

I was about to make a bloody great mess everywhere.

CHAPTER FOURTEEN

1,000 DAYS

And then I tried cocaine.

I can't really recall the first time I stuck it up my nose, other than it took place during the weeks, or maybe months after the Klitschko fight. I think somebody must have offered it to me. 'Pal,' they said, 'you want some of this?' And given that I didn't care about anything at the time, I dived in and spent the next two years chasing a feeling that didn't exist. It was horrible stuff, a load of shite, and I wouldn't recommend it to anyone. (The same goes for any drug.) Every morning after doing cocaine, I found myself in a far worse emotional state than I'd been in before, and if I could have given my younger self some advice it would have been this: *Just say no.*

By the spring of 2016, my downward spiral seemed to be increasing in velocity, though luckily I wasn't destroying myself financially like some people had done in my position. That's because I wasn't blowing loads of money on gambling, drinks and going out. Whenever I went partying, I wasn't showing up at the doors of London's hottest joints. I was going to a dive in Morecambe where a pint of beer cost around two quid. The worst part was the turmoil being inflicted upon Paris. It must have been horrible for her, seeing me falling apart in the way that I was.

Despite this, the world outside our family carried on as if everything was running smoothly; the boxing machine kept ticking over. In April 2016, it was announced that I would be fighting Klitschko again that summer and this time it would be at the Manchester Arena – home advantage. That meant *my* gloves, *my* scales, and *my* canvas. But the chances of me being ready for another heavyweight title contest were longer than a million-to-one shot and when a press conference was held to promote the event, I rocked up and acted like a crazy person. I even ripped off my shirt to reveal the consequences of several months spent on the piss and the pastry.

'Legacies don't mean a lot to me,' I said, as I began a speech that I have thought a lot about since. 'Boxing doesn't even mean much to me, otherwise I wouldn't go into camp four stone overweight every time, having eaten every pie in Lancashire and drunk every pint in the UK.'

Here comes the really weird part, though. 'I hate every second of training,' I continued. 'I hate boxing. I hate the lot. I hate speaking to you idiots. I'd rather be at home watching television and eating chocolate.' As you will know by now from reading this book, my words were completely out of character.

I turned to Klitschko and gestured to my belly. 'Does

that look like a fighter's body to you? No. *Shame on you.* You let a fat man beat you.'

Finally, I told the room what I really thought about my day job, the sport I'd spent my childhood fantasising about. 'I hate it, but I am too good at it to stop. I hope Klitschko knocks me out because I can then retire and go on holiday.'

In preparation for the fight, I went running in the Lake District and sprained my ankle. I must have slipped on a curb or a step and tripped over, and the Klitschko rematch was postponed. Whether I felt relieved or not is hard to remember, because I was lost in the fog of depression, unable to get a grip on what was happening and whether the events of my life really mattered. My guess is that I didn't care. When a person has lost the will to live it's not as if they're going to give a hoot about a boxing match.

While I fully own my destructive behaviour from this time, and I don't blame anyone but myself, I noticed something alarming in certain people around me during this period: they were clearly watching what was a slow-moving car crash and it wouldn't have taken a genius for one of them to work out that I was very unwell and falling apart at the seams. (Of course, this doesn't apply to Paris and a few close family and friends, who were my rocks.) Yet despite my very public breakdown, nobody stepped in to help. Not one person from boxing pulled me aside and asked me if I was OK.

Nobody wanted to know what was going on behind closed doors, or if I needed support or even advice. Boxing didn't seem to care if I was emotionally broken. It just wanted to see the rematch – *Fury v Klitschko II* – and my state of mind didn't seem to matter.

• • •

My head was on fire. I was spiralling out of control and at times I experienced intense panic attacks when my heart seemed ready to explode from my chest. At one point I even became convinced that my best friend Dave wanted to kill me, though that wasn't the case at all. Whenever I went to bed, I slept with the lights on because I would hear demons talking in the dark. I was afraid of the unknown and not seeing what was with me in the room created a sense of dread.

In my heaviest moments, I often thought about suicide, and then one morning, I decided to give it a go.* I opened

* If you are experiencing suicidal thoughts, please seek professional assistance immediately. Help is out there and I have put some resources at the back of the book. I hope my story is an example that brighter days are ahead. You too can make your comeback.

my eyes, hating what I'd become; wishing that I'd died in my sleep, knowing it was time to end it all. Later that day while driving around, I aimed my Ferrari at a bridge; with my feet pressed hard on the accelerator, the motor roaring, I knew that I was only a second or two away from a violent but blessed ending.

Then suddenly a voice called out.

Don't.

Don't do this.

Think of your children.

Don't let them grow up without a father.

Don't let them think that you killed yourself because you couldn't handle it.

At the last instant, I veered away from a devastating collision and slammed down on the brakes. I felt the car slowing, my heart racing, my soul knowing right then that I had to ask for support, because without it I was going to die and ruin the lives of everyone around me.

I need help, I thought. *Medical help.*

My problem was that I didn't know where to go, or what to do when it came to the matter of getting my head fixed. I had zero clues about mental health because in the Traveller culture we didn't talk about those issues. Admitting to depression, or some other psychological injury, was considered a sign of weakness. Even when I later opened up to my family about the emotional problems bringing me down, they didn't have a clue about what to do.

Up until that moment, I'd been in denial. I knew that something was wrong, I'd even said it out loud to people, but I didn't want to admit it to myself fully by asking for help. Doing so was the final step. In many ways I was like an alcoholic who had been drinking three bottles of vodka a day while making jokes about their addiction. Deep down I knew it was bad, but reaching out for support was scary because there was a stigma attached to issues of the mind; in reality, I had to treat my head in much the same way that I would have treated a broken leg or a leaking pipe in the house. In those situations I'd have called in the relevant specialist without giving it a second thought. My pain had to be considered in much the same way.

In the end, I did some online research and checked in with what I hoped would be the best people in the area. One of them was a psychiatrist in Preston where my problems were diagnosed. By the sounds of things I had the lot, but because of my paranoia and anxiety, I really didn't think the treatment they then suggested would be for me at first. I even became worried about what would happen in the sessions. In the days leading up to my first consultation I got it into my head that the doctor would inevitably go to the pub afterwards. A few pints in he was bound to gossip with his mates about my condition.

I could imagine the conversation that might take place, with everyone laughing at me. 'Yeah, I just had Tyson Fury in my office. *The heavyweight champion of the world?* He told me all these things; he's got all these problems . . . What a baby he is.'

That might be the reaction in some people when they meet a famous individual through work – they gossip with their mates about the encounter later on down the line. But the stakes aren't usually so great in those situations because the information being shared isn't as intensely personal. In my frazzled state I assumed a doctor would do the same, not knowing that he or she was under a legal obligation to protect my information. In the end I put my fears to one side and went anyway, because what other option did I have? It soon turned out to be the right move. For the first session, I showed up with my dad and brothers and after a couple of appointments I realised the work was becoming helpful, though there would be no silver bullet to my condition.

In crisis, I learned a lot about myself. During one appointment, the doctor drew a line graph on a whiteboard. It was broken up with the occasional peak and trough. 'This is how a healthy person's life looks,' he said.

Then he drew another line. This time, the peaks and troughs were so extreme and frequent that the graph resembled the top of Bart Simpson's head. 'And, Tyson, this is what your life looks like.'

He then explained my condition would need medication, but that I would be OK. Apparently I was like a lot of other people because mental health issues were very common. 'You've bottled up your problems for so long that you've had a meltdown,' he said.

Clearly, there was a lot of work to be done.

At first I was placed on a suicide watch, where a psychiatrist explained how I'd been held together by my faith in God. Without it, they reckoned, I'd have made a successful job of killing myself.

'But it ain't going to hold you together for ever,' they said.

As the work progressed, I started to realise how impactful my behaviour had been and that I'd so nearly wrecked the lives of everyone in my family. Driving into that bridge at top speed wouldn't just have ended my life. It would have destroyed Paris's and the kids' too.

'How could I be that person?' I thought. 'How could I do that? How could I be so selfish?'

That was a terrifying realisation, but at least it was something. Feeling pain meant that I was healing at least. In the past few years there had been long periods when I hadn't felt anything at all.

• • •

I'm sure it wasn't easy for Paris, being married to a twenty-something Jack the Lad; one who thought he was good-looking and was fast turning into a boxing champion.

The first nine rounds against John McDermott were a bruising grind but I hung in there, biding my time, taking shots whenever I could. My head wobbled, my body stiffened, but I managed to stay strong and cuffed him about the head a few times.

Against McDermott I had to bite down on my gumshield to stay in. It wasn't my best performance, but I showed enough grit and determination to pull through, so I was happy.

My first-ever pro appearance in the US, fighting Steve Cunningham in Madison Square Garden.

I knocked him out in the seventh round and my ambition soared: 'If I can make it here, I can make it anywhere . . .'

To work my way towards the top dog, I had to beat Derek Chisora. I jabbed his ears off over twelve rounds, winning on a unanimous decision. I was twenty-two years old. Finally the world was coming to understand that I was destined for greatness.

Beating Wladimir Klitschko was probably my most spectacular moment in the ring because, firstly, it showed the world what I was truly capable of and, secondly, it was so utterly against the odds that not many people could believe it had actually happened.

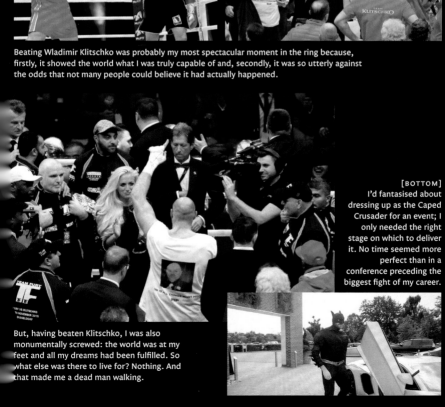

But, having beaten Klitschko, I was also monumentally screwed: the world was at my feet and all my dreams had been fulfilled. So what else was there to live for? Nothing. And that made me a dead man walking.

[BOTTOM] I'd fantasised about dressing up as the Caped Crusader for an event; I only needed the right stage on which to deliver it. No time seemed more perfect than in a conference preceding the biggest fight of my career.

My draw with Wilder in our first fight proved that, no matter what life chucked at a person, it was possible to withstand the punishment.

I'd given Wilder the toughest battle of his career so far.

After Wilder, I fought Schwarz. Nothing he could throw at me could connect. I punished him in double quick time and demolished him.

I knew that, if I could come through and defeat Wallin, my next fight was going to be a rematch with Wilder. With an incentive like that, no one was going to stop me.

Even as a blood-splattered mess, I won on a unanimous decision.

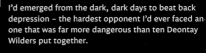

For weeks before our rematch, Wilder had been chatting about how I'd thrown soft punches in our first fight. Apparently they were like feather dusters. But on the night, they didn't seem so soft and fluffy, and Wilder didn't appear so ballsy.

I'd emerged from the dark, dark days to beat back depression – the hardest opponent I'd ever faced and one that was far more dangerous than ten Deontay Wilders put together.

Me at my lowest. I weighed around 28 stone.

My fitness improved and the comeback was on.

The recovery was brutal. With my new coach, Ben Davison, I hammered myself into the ground to get fit and emotionally well again. For a few months, Ben even moved into the Fury family home and I trained with him every day, twice a day, as I worked on getting back in shape.

[TOP] I'm lucky to have a great support team in the gym. We train hard but we also have a lot of fun.

Exercise has become so important to me that I don't even consider it a hobby anymore – it is more a human function, like breathing or eating.

I've been a huge wrestling fan all my life, starting from when the likes of The Rock, Stone Cold Steve Austin and Bret 'The Hitman' Hart reigned supreme.

I recently sponsored my local football club, Morecambe F.C. I also have a gym space there, only a couple of miles away from the house.

Once you've stared death in the eyes and somehow walked away in one piece, you'll have an idea of just how precious every moment on this earth is. The time is short too, so grab it by the bollocks. Because The Gypsy King did and he became the undefeated champion of his dream life. And, trust me, he's still loving it.

While all of this had been going on, the United Kingdom Anti-Doping (UKAD) charged my cousin Hughie and me, claiming to have found elevated levels of the banned substance nandrolone in our systems. I can tell you right now that I have never taken a performance-enhancing drug in my life. But UKAD claimed that my results from a February 2015 urine test, after my fight with Christian Hammer, had shown higher levels of nandrolone than normal. (It's produced naturally by the body and reduces tiredness and helps muscle growth.) For a while, it looked as if I was going to be suspended, but that was eventually lifted after an appeal and I was free to carry on fighting once the matter was resolved in 2017.

Following my ankle injury, a new date for the Klitschko fight was set for October 2016, again at the Manchester Arena, and the boxing machine put me through the wheels once more. I wasn't having any of it, though. When another press conference with Klitschko was arranged in London that September, nobody informed me until the night before. Why I'm not sure, but I wasn't exactly pleased.

'I'm not doing it,' I said. Which as you know by now, wasn't like me. I love a press conference. I just wasn't in the right state of mind.

Whoever told me had looked shocked.

When the press conference kicked off the next day, my manager Mick Hennessy told the room that my car had broken down and the battery in my phone had died.

The same could be said of my boxing career. I was forced to withdraw from the Klitschko rematch, not for fighting reasons, but for medical ones. My head wasn't up to it. The statement was delivered by Mick Hennessy:

> *Medical specialists have advised that the condition is too severe to allow him to participate in the rematch and that he will require treatment before going back into the ring. Tyson will now immediately undergo the treatment he needs to make a full recovery. We and Tyson wish to express our sincerest apologies to all those concerned with the event and all the boxing fans who had been looking forward to the rematch. Tyson is understandably devastated by the development.*

A couple of weeks later, I delivered an interview with *Rolling Stone* magazine in which I told the journalist that I hoped somebody killed me before I was able to kill myself. I even claimed it would be my last interview. Before long I'd given up my WBA, WBO and IBO titles.

I was done.

• • •

Despite seeing a psychiatrist, I still drank and partied hard, though at least I was now imagining a time when I might turn the corner. I'd go to the pub and sink ten pints, while convincing myself I was going back to training the following morning. But when the hangover inevitably kicked in, I'd put my boxing comeback on hold for a little while longer. During 2017, my life felt like a never-ending season of false dawns. Then, in October I ended up at a Halloween party, dressed in a skeleton outfit, so nobody knew who I was, with yet another pint of beer in my hand.

But a switch was flipped.

It was like I'd experienced a moment of clarity. As I looked about the room, I saw university students, kids at the beginning of their lives. And here I was, a grown man, the former heavyweight world champion, with a wife and family, drinking myself silly.

You've been at the pinnacle of your career, I thought. *And you've chucked it all away. What's going on? What are you doing here?*

I put my pint down and went home. I walked upstairs, took off the stupid skeleton outfit and dropped to my knees. Then I prayed to God and cried like a baby.

'I can't do this anymore,' I said. 'I've had enough of this life. I can't do it on my own. If there's any way back to boxing for me, please bring me back, because I can't take life without boxing.'

With hindsight, that party was a turning point for me – 100 per cent. In those blurry moments in the pub, as I took in the scene, I had a moment of sanity. I realised I shouldn't have been there. *I should have been at home.* And there's no doubt that the realisation started my healing process. Whether I would have still arrived at that point had I not gone to a party dressed in a skeleton costume is a whole other matter for debate. You never know what's down for your life or what might be around the corner.

What I do know is that a bookie doing the odds on a Tyson Fury comeback would have taken one look at me and laughed. I weighed around 28 stone. I'd had my boxing licence suspended by the British Boxing Board of Control after a psychiatrist had deemed me medically unfit to fight.

The following morning I got out of bed, pulled on my sweat suit and went for a jog. My plan was to run a mile out and a mile back, but as my trainers hammered the pavement I realised my body couldn't do it. I was that fat and knackered. Talk about demoralising. As I strolled back to the house, having done half of what I was hoping, I pulled out my phone and scrolled through social media. I don't know why but I went to Deontay Wilder's page. As I moved down the screen, I saw a post in which he said he'd seen a picture of me. He was declaring me finished. A little further down he reckoned it was a shame that we'd never fought one another. Wilder also reckoned he could punch Mike Tyson out in one round.

That pissed me off. Unknowingly, he had lit a firework underneath me. *For those comments, I'm going to come back and I'm going to knock you spark out*, I thought.

At that time, there had been all sorts of toing and froing between Anthony Joshua and Wilder over a potential fight.

Will they, won't they?

They are. They're not.

He said. She said.

It had been boring on for about a year. I knew then I was taking the bull by the horns.

'Joshua ain't got the bollocks to do it, so it's going to take an old, fat, bald-headed feller to come out of retirement — nearly three years out of the game — to beat Deontay Wilder.'

The comeback of all comebacks had begun.

• • •

A quick footnote before we move on: If there was one positive from my breakdown it was the very public nature of it. It showed me as being mortal. Yeah, I was unwell and hurting, but I'd needed to go through that experience to become the man I am today. What I hope is that there are some people who will look and learn from my experience. And know this: there's nothing wrong in asking for help. It saved my life. It might save yours, or the life of someone you love.

CHAPTER FIFTEEN

THE SECOND COMING

At the beginning of November, still fired up by Deontay Wilder's social media post, I called the personal trainer, Ben Davison. If you don't know this story already, we first met at a boxing show in Glasgow during 2016. Fast-forward a year and Ben was in Marbella working on the fitness levels of my pal, the middleweight Billy Joe Saunders, as he prepared to defend his WBO title. I went over to visit and even did a little training, despite my hating boxing at the time. While there, Ben and me had hit it off and when I decided to make a return to the ring in 2018, I knew he was the man to get me back in shape.

Having asked him, Ben moved into the Fury family's Morecambe house where we started a six-week fitness programme. We then flew out to another training camp in Marbella in January 2018 and in the process, I dropped a tonne of weight. I had the spark again, the old Tyson Fury was coming back to life, and Ben was very much behind the transformation. It helped that he was a young lad, only in his mid twenties at the time, and without the commitment of a wife or kids. He was able to work with me whenever and wherever I wanted without too much disruption. Our working relationship had clicked, like I sensed it would.

The fact that Ben hadn't yet trained another boxer to a belt wasn't a concern either. (He would later help Billy Joe to defend that first WBO title.) That's because I didn't need the world's greatest coaching minds behind me to win boxing matches. I only required someone with enough knowledge to steer me in the right direction. Ben was a mate, that was the most important thing, and I didn't need someone screaming at me, or a ball-breaker, because I've never responded positively to that style of coaching. I wanted someone to help me back to my old self and have a laugh at the same time. Credit to him, Ben managed it, and in the space of eight months or so, I shifted ten stone.

Despite this brutal change, Ben's training was fun. The sparring sessions that had been so self-destructive during my darker days became pleasurable again, but that's because I was finding my way back to an emotionally stronger spot. I had purpose. My aim was to fight at the top level, the place where I belonged, rather than being a fat mess looking on from the sidelines. The work was life-changing too, and since those days of training with Ben in 2018, I don't think I've had a week out of the gym. The upgraded Tyson Fury was a different animal.

My fire was back — and knowing that inspired me to work even harder. As I kept improving bit by bit I never once rested on my laurels, because I was constantly looking for more. That's how greatness is forged, especially in a sport like boxing. A fighter that settles for mediocrity never fulfils their true potential. Meanwhile, having already won the world heavyweight title, there was nothing more I needed to achieve, and nothing left to lose, because I had lost it all already. With no fixed objectives in the distance to obsess over (as I had done with Klitschko) I was able to soak up everything that was happening. And I appreciated it all, understanding that nothing lasts for ever, the good and the bad.

I wasn't yet out of the woods with regards to my mental health though. While I was undoubtedly getting better with each passing month, the demons were proving hard to shake off. I continued sleeping with the light on, but that was happening because I was still suffering from anxiety and feeling uncertain of what the future might bring, whereas depression, from what I could tell, was partly the result of having past regrets. Still, I was happy to press ahead with my punishing fitness regime, knowing that I'd become engaged in a lifelong battle to stay emotionally healthy. No matter what people say about mental illnesses – the type of which I was suffering – recovery is an ongoing process, in much the same way that an alcoholic or a junkie is never really cured of their addictions. Every day is going to be a fight. I've had to keep my problems at bay with a long, stiff jab.

That was a hard pill to swallow at first, but I've long known that the most valuable things in life arrive after a bit of a scrap. Easy was going to the pub on the daily. Easy was eating every bag of chips in sight. Easy was whacking on ten stone. Hard was getting my head straight, as was returning to the fitness levels I'd enjoyed when duffing up the likes of Klitschko and Derek Chisora. Annoyingly, being healthy requires a lot of motivation and discipline. If it didn't, we'd all be walking around shredded, able to run a 20-miler without breaking sweat. Not that I was interested in either of those things because I had found a much more powerful motivator. My mental fortitude was everything.

• • •

While my return to fitness gathered pace and I went through the process of getting my suspended boxing licence *unsuspended*, it felt as if a weird wall of silence had gone up around the world of boxing. I noticed that very few people gave a damn about me. I certainly don't remember too many people from the sport calling me to check if I was OK, even after my very public withdrawal from the Klitschko fight and that infamous *Rolling Stone* interview. I realised once again that when a boxer is doing well, as I had been for several years, certain people are happy to stick their hands out for money. But when that same athlete is down on their luck, badly injured, or at the end of their career, those figures don't seem to care.

I was in a unique position. For a brief while, I had stood at the top of the boxing ladder and experienced how the game worked. On the way up, people wanted to talk to me. They tried to offer me new opportunities and deals. They acted like they cared. But in the spring of 2018, having rag-dolled to the bottom of the ladder and been as close to death as a person could get without the game being over, I found the experience to be so very different. The opportunities and deals dried up. My phone never rang. Because of my breakdown, I was out in the cold.

This poor treatment didn't bother me while I was in the thick of my issues, because I'd been willing to meet my maker at the time. So if I didn't care about my life, or the people around me, I was hardly going to care about how people viewed me or my business. That said, once I'd got into a better place, I realised that boxing had nothing in the way of aftercare for a person like me, and that was a problem. For a time, I'd found myself in serious trouble, but there was nobody in the sport to turn to for help. There were no therapists or experts to lean upon. My experience was that fighters were used and abused and then kicked to the kerb. The attitude from the money grabbers in those situations seemed to be very clear: 'Never mind. We'll feast off the next one.'

I've made this point in the past, but it bears repeating because it's an important issue: this attitude isn't just confined to boxing. In a number of sports where physical sacrifices are made and personal safety is put on the line (and in services like the military) people work hard for their careers. Then, when that chapter in their life comes to an unexpected close, or they experience a serious injury, they are immediately thrown onto the scrap heap. For those individuals whose fortunes are being played out in the public eye, the situation can feel even more intense because, suddenly, everyone has an opinion on their demise. A track-and-field champ can be deemed worthless overnight, even though they were doing well a year or so previously. A Premier League footballer might be branded as 'rubbish', despite having played for their country. Once finished, those people discover that nobody wants to know them anymore. That is a very lonely and triggering place to be, especially if they are emotionally vulnerable.

My situation was a little different in that I had a chance of returning to the very top. If I did, I promised to remember the individuals that had forgotten me so easily. And I would never attend one of their fancy dinners or awards presentations again.

• • •

To get my boxing licence back, I had to prove I was both emotionally strong and physically ready. To do so I visited the same psychiatrist that had previously declared me medically unfit after withdrawing from the Klitschko fight. In the end, I was judged to be in good enough shape to compete again. The British Boxing Board of Control reinstated my licence. This followed the conclusion of my dispute with UKAD over the detected nandrolone levels in my system. The process had gone on for a couple of years.

With my return to the world stage confirmed I only had to figure out who to fight and when. Frank Warren first lined up the Albanian Sefer Seferi and the stage for my second coming was set. Seferi was fairly unknown at the time, having previously fought in the cruiserweight division, and wasn't considered as being too dangerous. The tale of the tape wasn't worrying either: he was ten years older, six inches shorter, and nearly five stones lighter. (My reach was ten inches longer too.) But on the other hand, Seferi had been in twenty-four fights and only lost once. He also had a good knockout ratio. As far as I was concerned he was a solid opponent for my first fight in three years.

The match wasn't about the opponent though; it was all about my return to the ring and when the Manchester Arena was announced as the venue, *home turf*, 15,000 tickets were sold. Thankfully, lots of people still wanted to see The Gypsy King up close. As the date approached, I felt like a fish cooped up in a tank. I wanted to be released into the ocean where I belonged. Though, weirdly, I think Seferi was just as excited as me. He asked for so many pictures during the build-up to the fight that, for a while, I wondered whether I'd been his hero at some point. He was getting paid a lot of money to fight me as well. As long as he got out of the ring in one piece, Seferi was going to be OK.

Given my breakdown had been so messy and public, there was a chance I was going to take a bit of stick from my opponents in the coming fights, but I wasn't worried. (During my second career, I can only really recall Deontay Wilder saying anything, and I can't remember what exactly, so it can't have been that bad.) Seferi didn't behave in that way, though he probably didn't know what to expect from our fight. There's a chance he might have considered me to be way past my best, as a lot of people did.

Certainly a large percentage of boxing fans and fighters were probably underestimating my chances of making a significant comeback beyond Seferi, but that was nothing new. In my first career, opponents judged me on my body shape as if that was any indication of what I could, or couldn't, do in the ring. They took one look at me and thought, 'He's an overweight bloke . . . There's no way he can fight.' Yeah, I might have appeared slow, clumsy and horrible from a distance. But after thirty seconds close up, whoever was trapped in the ring with me usually uncovered a very unpleasant truth: going against The Gypsy King is like trying to carry a two-ton weight to the summit of Everest.

The thing is, I've never been bothered about how I appear, or how people perceive my image. Some fighters fuss over their style; they look chiselled, as if they've been cut from granite, but they are more like male models than warriors. I am not one of those blokes – and I'm very happy about it, thank you very much. I love having a dad bod; I'm good with my love handles. When people imagine a heavy-weight champion of the world, they usually picture a cut, athletic-looking dude. They never consider a person who looks like me, which is a mistake because The Gypsy King can fight like an animal.

The same goes for my hair. I much prefer being bald to those times in my younger days when I had a bunch of curly locks sprouting from my skull. Most of the time, I looked like a big mop head, and the style became a real mess whenever I fought – with each landed punch, my fringe flew all over the place, which created the impression that I'd been really hit, especially when it was sweaty. After a while I shaved it off because I like being bald, not because I want to intimidate my opponents. That isn't my style. I'm all about having fun.

The Seferi fight was a good example of that attitude.

On the night of the fight, I gave him a peck on the lips as we bumped gloves at the start of the fight. The commentators couldn't believe what they were seeing. But I knew I had to make an immediate impression. The sport had become mind-numbing in my absence, like it had been during the reign of Klitschko. In the build-up to every fight, two boxers stepped into the press conference and shook hands, or wished one another good luck. But everyone was being too respectful. *Where was the fire and lightning?* Boxing is a form of show business. With my return it was going to be like a circus again.

I walked out to a mash-up of famous comeback hits – LL Cool J's 'Mama Said Knock You Out' and 'Without Me' by Eminem – the DJ following up by making a knowing nod to my breakdown with Afroman's hit, 'Because I Got High'. Once 'Return of the Mack' by Mark Morrison had kicked in, the crowd was left in little doubt that I was hoping to pick up from where I left off. A chant ricocheted around the seats. *'One Tyson Fury! There's only one Tyson Fury. One Tyson Fury . . .'* After all my struggles, it felt extra sweet to be back. I was exactly where I wanted to be. I fed off the crowd and they gave me all the energy I needed.

The fun and games really began once the fight was underway. I worked out very quickly that Seferi was there for the taking whenever I fancied it, but I needed a few rounds under my belt. The quality of opponent was only going to increase in the coming contests, so the longer the bout went on, the better it was for me: I needed to find my match legs again and to box away any rustiness. I let him come at me in the first, pulling faces at the crowd as he did so – I was fully in control of the situation. I put my hands above my head and invited him on; I danced across the canvas and at one point I even feinted to throw a hay-maker. Then I drew a telling off from the ref for pirouet-ting 360 degrees in the ring and making a comment or two to the crowd. He'd clearly seen enough of the horseplay, so I loomed over Seferi with every attack. By round three I was landing some heavy punches and as soon as I knuckled down and threw a couple of solid hits, it was game over. Seferi retired in his corner before the fifth.

The comeback was on. A few months later, I defeated the Italian Francesco Pianeta to complete one of the most thrilling returns in sporting history. I'd survived an emotional meltdown, the vacating of my belts and a suicide attempt to make it back to the world of professional boxing. It also felt as if people wanted to see me succeed again. That might have been because I was now more like the average person on the street than a supreme athlete – one of those chiselled model-types I mentioned earlier. Instead I resem-bled the average Joe, the sort of person you might see prop-ping up the bar in your local boozer, with all his flaws and problems. I suppose that vulnerability and normality had captured the public's imagination. Because when they looked at me, they probably found it hard not to see a little bit of themselves.

· · ·

A boxing legend was working alongside Ben Davison in my corner for those first two comeback fights: Ricky 'The Hitman' Hatton, the former world champion in both the welterweight and light welterweight divisions. I first met Ricky before he became a top fighter, at a boxing show, in a working mans' club in Sale. He was an amateur at the time. In fact, it was so early on his career that people referred to him as Richard – the 'Ricky' and 'Hitman' monikers would come later on. I could only have been eleven years old. Because the show was taking place in those days before the smoking ban had kicked in, a cloud of cigarette smoke swirled about the venue like a pea soup fog.

After that night, Ricky quickly became one of my favourite boxers. In fact, I'd go as far as to call him one of my childhood heroes. I watched all his fights on the telly because he was fearless and ferocious, he wasn't intimidated by anybody and I loved the way he used to get stuck in. The Hitman was a natural entertainer.

He was also one of the few people in boxing to have reached out to me when I became seriously ill. I had bumped into him in Manchester one night at a time when I was as big as a house.

'You should get back into training,' said Ricky and we swapped numbers.

From time to time, he would check in to see if I was OK, which was appreciated because I knew that he'd gone through some serious health problems of his own. In 2010, Ricky was reportedly admitted to The Priory rehab centre due to his struggle with booze and depression. After we'd met, I saw some videos of him smashed, falling over, and not looking too good, so I returned the favour and called him to see if he was OK.

'Look, if you need any help or whatever, give us a call,' I said. 'If you need any advice, let me know. I've been through it all myself.'

Before the Seferi and Pianeta contests, I was training out of Ricky's gym in Manchester. I saw Ricky all the time and we got very pally, to the point where I reckoned he would be a good addition to my team.

'Do you want to come into the corner?' I said.

Ricky loved the idea. It was good to have him in there with me for moral support. Having a legend of the game to back me up from time to time felt reassuring. And with a childhood hero in my corner, the future felt bright.

CHAPTER SIXTEEN

THE KING OF AMERICA

There was business to be done. As those defeats of Seferi and Pianeta were taking place, the talk had turned to the identity of my next opponent. A lot of chat was flying around about this fighter and that, but I could only think of one person I wanted to pound into the canvas. The man at the top; the dosser in my seat; the fella who had taken to social media to make comments about my withdrawal from the arena: Deontay Wilder.

When I'd signed with Frank Warren our deal had originally been for five scheduled fights, but by the time I'd defeated Pianeta, I was already getting impatient with just boxing. I wanted to be the best again, and to get there I needed a title bout. If I went for it and turned out not to be good enough, well at least I'd tried.

'Frank, get that fight with Wilder,' I said.

He wasn't convinced. 'Are you sure?'

Of course I was sure. I always jumped in at the deep end. 'Yeah, get it over the line.'

'It's probably too soon,' he warned. 'Maybe you should have another year, another couple of fights at least . . . Before you go for Wilder—'

'Get it done.'

Fair play to Frank, he pulled it together and once both parties had broken bread a deal was struck: *Fury v Wilder* was to take place at the Staples Center in LA on 1 December 2018. At the time, I imagine Wilder's people had accepted me as enough of a high-profile face for their boy to beat up. They probably thought, 'He's a big name, but he's been out of the ring for three years, so how good can he be? He's been abusing himself. He can't be superhuman . . .' It is also known that returning lineal champions have a tendency for getting dropped, especially ones that had been away for as long as me. And let's not forget Wilder was an absolute beast. Prior to our first meeting, he'd successfully defended the WBC heavyweight title seven times after first winning it against Bermane Stiverne in 2015, dropping the undefeated Gerald Washington and Luis Ortiz along the way. So of course they were confident, but little did they know that I was no ordinary lineal champion.

I still needed an upgraded fitness regime to take on a fighter of Wilder's standing, so to prepare we flew to California and The Summit Gym – the world-famous Big Bear Lake training camp in the San Bernardino Mountains, where I worked at high altitude. The base was designed in the 1990s by the boxing trainer Abel Sanchez, and the first visitors were Lennox Lewis and his trainer (and mine), the late Manny Steward, though a lot of big fighters would prepare there over the years, including Oscar De La Hoya and Shane Mosley. It was a great place to work: there were no distractions and everybody stayed in log cabins. Despite the idyllic surroundings, my four-week stint at increased altitude proved eye-opening. We worked at 2,100 metres above sea level and the training was hard; the thin air burned my lungs and there was a concern in some sections of the camp that I was struggling. But it wasn't wise to underestimate The Gypsy King. When we later worked out at a sea level, in a town called Ontario, it turned out that I was fit as a fiddle.

Having powered through four gruelling weeks we later moved down to Hollywood, which delivered a little slice of glamour. That feeling only increased when I realised our gym was stationed off the famous Walk of Fame where the stars had their names branded across the sidewalk. The gym we used was owned by Freddie Roach, the trainer famous for working with the likes of Manny Pacquiao, Julio César Chávez Jr and Amir Khan, and after a while, my schedule became almost therapeutic. In the mornings, I often ran around the nearby reservoir during a five-mile jog, taking in the instantly recognisable Hollywood sign ahead and soaking up the nature around me — deer, hummingbirds and all.

During this period in my life I was coming to the realisation that good chats and banter during training was an incredible form of healing for me. This feeling had started almost from the minute Ben and I began working together, but it helped that a boxing camp was as a good place as any to talk about whatever was going on in my head. Blokes are notoriously bad at expressing themselves, or sharing the issues in their lives. But when surrounded by good people in a working environment, I could chat to the others for hours on end about our ambitions and hopes, and where we wanted to be in four or five years' time. There was plenty of opportunity to natter too, because so much time was spent recovering between sessions. I discovered that the gym was a positive environment for me to be suffering in. Good company, along with exercise, was becoming my special tonic and I wanted to take it daily.

In the opening phase of my second career, training had mainly concentrated on weight loss. Getting in shape for Seferi and Pianeta had required me to shift the equivalent of a whole other bloke in pounds – albeit a small one. But for the Wilder fight I needed to alter my focus; tactics and strength were now in play because my opponent was such a dangerous puncher. That didn't mean I was fully primed: despite my hard work in California, I was yet to hit peak power and nowhere near ready for a fighter of his calibre. But I was getting there. (Let me tell you, losing ten stone in a year was debilitating.) In that respect, while fighting Wilder was a courageous move, it was also a bloody dangerous one. I was taking a gamble with my life.

Boom! The gamble paid off. As I described earlier in this book, I earned an against-the-odds draw against Wilder in a fight for the ages and everything changed again. I scored a massive American deal with the Cable TV company, ESPN, and the promoters, Top Rank; from then on I was taken to America so I could be filmed and featured properly — the days of being used and abused, as I had been during my first career, seemed over. Though I hadn't yet overcome the man with most of my belts, my recovery story was a headline-grabber and it unexpectedly helped to restore my top biller status. I bought a house in Vegas within a gated community because the plan once *Fury v Wilder II* had been officially announced was to make Sin City a base. In the end, I only ever went there to train, or to ready myself whenever a fight was taking place. People used to ask me, 'How can you train in Vegas?' I told them: 'Easily. I get up, go to the gym and eat. Then I train again, eat, and go to bed.' I was never there to party or mess about.

It also helped that the American crowds really took to me whenever I showed up. In our first fight I'd given Wilder the toughest battle of his career so far. I later put on a show during the Otto Wallin match in Vegas on Mexican Independence Day in September 2019, when my eyebrow cracked open and blood and thunder spilled out over the canvas — I must have looked like a battle-scarred extra from *Game of Thrones*. Looking back now, I doubt America had seen a Brit as arrogant, charismatic and loud-mouthed as me. Yeah, American fighters play that game all the time. But when someone from the UK tried the same tactic they were generally smashed to smithereens in the ring afterwards.

I was an exception to the rule, firstly because I didn't sound like Hugh Grant, and secondly because my attitude towards show business chimed with the American market. As a boxer, my job was to entertain. I also wanted to be successful, which the US audience found incredibly exciting. They love winners; they don't mind their athletes wandering about in diamond-encrusted gold chains, or driving their Rollers through town. They say, 'Oh, man, you worked so hard for that car. You're an inspiration!' That is so very different to the attitude in Britain, where if someone is flashy and confident they are categorised as being a prick, and a bloke driving a Roller is called a Rolls-Royce Wanker.

So no way did I want to come across as being boring when fighting in Vegas. To behave like a Wladimir Klitschko or an Anthony Joshua would have been a wasted opportunity, especially as I'd finally returned to the top level. Instead I was making the most of my time in the limelight. And if people wanted to call me a wanker for driving a fancy car, well, that was entirely up to them.

• • •

Then the World Wrestling Entertainment Inc stepped in.

Shortly after the Otto Wallin fight they called and asked if I fancied taking on their star wrestler, Braun Strowman – AKA The Monster Among Men – at the WWE Crown Jewel in Saudi Arabia. I only had one answer to that, and it was, *Hell, yeah!* Then I remembered my physical condition. While I was fighting fit and revved up for a rematch against Wilder (where I was definitely going to obliterate him), my right eye was still healing from that bloody fight with Wallin.

What the hell, I thought. *I'm going to do it anyway.*

No way was I going to miss out on such a great opportunity. For one, I'd been a huge wrestling fan all my life, starting from when the likes of The Rock, Stone Cold Steve Austin and Bret 'The Hitman' Hart reigned supreme. I also guessed that wrestling could be taught, and I fancied my chances at picking up some of the moves. Plus the sport suited my personality – I was super outgoing, confident, and willing to have a go at something new. Given all of that, taking on Strowman would be a chance for me to test my skills in a different arena while cranking up my visibility in America even more. For a while, it was impossible to turn on the telly without seeing The Gypsy King's face, what with my fights against Wilder, Wallin, Schwarz and the forthcoming *Fury v Wilder II* showdown, plus a WWE battle. I was the Jamie Oliver of American pay-per-view.

The training lasted a month and bloody hell it was brutal. Anyone who criticises the 'fake' style of pro wrestling is talking out of their arse and for four weeks I was slammed down on the canvas, for hours on end. This isn't the type of canvas preferred by Wladimir Klitschko and his boys either; it is a hard surface. That didn't put me off. I took my time and I worked hard, because I was determined to put on a great show. It helped that I was match fit, what with my fight schedule, though I ended every session covered in bruises and burns. But no way was I going to skip the effort. I didn't want to look a carrot when making my wrestling debut. The pain was a price worth paying.

For my entrance to the fight, I dressed in a Saudi thawb and traditional headdress, walking through the crowd to the sound of The Isley Brothers song, 'It's Your Thing' as a TV commentator gave me a fitting intro. *Well, ladies and gentlemen, anyone who has followed the career of Tyson Fury will know that this is vintage Tyson Fury. He is a bundle of charisma. He is outspoken. He is controversial. And he always wants to be on the main stage. And don't forget he also has some of the fastest hands of anybody to have stepped into a boxing ring. Six foot nine, hard-hitting, Tyson Fury. Don't be fooled by the charisma and the appearance — this is a bad, bad man.*

The battle was exhausting. Having jumped into the ring with Strowman, the pair of us had a real go at one another.

He was a big bloke, a little shorter than me, but a lot heavier, and everything you saw in the match was physically taxing. I hit Strowman with a running dropkick and before long, all the kicking and jumping had knackered me out, even though I was feeling fit after all those fights. Of course, we weren't dropping bombs on one another's heads, but I had to be careful because it wasn't uncommon for a wrestler to leave the ring with a broken neck, back or arms. My other concern was that eye injury, because with *Fury v Wilder II* looming on the horizon, I didn't want to have any weaknesses in my game. So I knocked Strowman out of the ring with a big right to win on a countout. There may have been a script for some parts of my wrestling smackdown, but The Gypsy King never loses.

• • •

If America thought they had seen the limits of my showmanship at the WWE Crown Jewel, then my reputation as a top-drawer showman was amplified even further when I then defeated Deontay Wilder in Vegas in 2020. Around 6,000 people showed up for the weigh-in, with thousands more locked outside the doors. Then thousands and thousands packed into the seats for the fight — it felt like a proper showbiz event as Vegas was overrun with boxing fans. The intense interest was unsurprising: this was a showdown between two undefeated world champions as they went toe-to-toe for the WBC title and the vacant *Ring* belt. But really, so much more was on the line.

That had everything to do with my struggles. Prior to *Fury v Wilder I*, I told a journalist from *The Sporting News* that I was fast becoming an unofficial ambassador for mental health. My attitude was that if the heavyweight champion of the world could admit to having problems, then anybody could do it.

'There's help around the corner,' I said. 'And it will get better, and I stand for that. I fight for those people.'

My draw with Wilder lent that attitude a greater power — it proved that no matter what life chucked at a person, it was possible to withstand the punishment. And even when every moment felt grey, there were always sunshine days ahead.

I took that same attitude into the sequel. Standing up to Wilder and not losing was one thing, but I knew that if I could beat him in *Fury v Wilder II* then it would deliver an even greater sense of hope. It was also important for me to speak up at that time, because despite my successes I was no different to anyone else. Depression wasn't kinder or crueller to me because of my status. It doesn't care who it hurts and anyone lost in the fog of mental health issues feels the same pain, whether they are the king or queen of their country, or the road sweeper outside the palace gates. Maybe I would have had an easier life had I kept my problems to my inner circle, but I wanted to inspire others, so I talked about it in every interview I did from then on. Once I'd beaten Wilder, the amount of people that stopped me in the street to say thanks for sharing my story was unbelievable. It was a very humbling experience.

At the same time, during that period it became important that I didn't entirely sacrifice my own emotional well-being while trying to help others. That came to the fore in 2021, after beating Wilder again in our third and final fight. I was on a high, but I knew to watch out for the trappings of success and acclaim. I took Robbie Williams' advice and became cautious about contracting Paradise Syndrome, so rather than taking time off, or allowing myself too much space to think, I set myself a routine from the minute I returned to Morecambe. I did the daily chores and trained hard in the gym. Getting up for a run every morning became something to look forward to as I went to bed at night. With a hectic schedule I was able to keep my demons at bay. It was a far cry from those grim days of 2015 to 2018. No lie, I'd have been suicidal within six months to a year if I hadn't put those routines in place.

That mindset had kept me alive during those three fights with Wilder, and it has also helped me since my 2022 Wembley fight with Dillian Whyte. Whether I fully walk away from the sport or not in the months or years to come, exercise has became so important to me that I don't even consider it a hobby anymore – it is more a human func-tion, like breathing or eating – and with every session, I feel the surge of serotonin lifting me up. It is as addictive as any high on the planet and I need a fix, twice a day. If I don't get it, I am like a junkie crawling the walls, the only difference being that this is a healthy habit, and one I have no intention of kicking. My grandfather on my mum's side used to run every day up until the moment he passed at the age of seventy-seven. He even went on a run during his last ever morning, so I have no excuse for not showing up.

But as I've said publicly before, depression is a little bit like the Hotel California, as made famous by The Eagles in their hit single of the same name: *I can check out, but I can never leave*. While training acts as a preventative measure, it isn't the cure, because there isn't one. I still have dark thoughts, but they are becoming less and less overwhelm-ing, and that's because I understand what they are and why they are happening. I also have the tools to work past them. The Tyson Fury of his first career had no clue about how to do that, which made depression a very scary adversary. The Tyson Fury of his second career is taking one day at a time and making sure to live in every moment.

I do that by keeping busy from the minute I get up in the morning to the moment my head hits the pillow. But in a weird contradiction, I've stopped making too many plans; I allow everything to become more spontaneous. I don't set dates on my calendar for holidays or get-togethers because I want those moments of happiness to happen off the cuff. Let me tell you, no bank balance or title belt has ever prevented a person from becoming mentally or physically unwell. Health and love is everything.

In many ways, every day feels like a gift and as a result I am as grateful for the big things in life as I am for the small, like a day out with my family, a cold drink in the sun, or the fresh sea air in Morecambe Bay. Previously I'd taken all of that for granted because everything had come so easily. I set goals; I hit them and that created a dangerous illusion where I believed everything would stay the same way for ever. But it wouldn't – *it couldn't* – as proven by those long periods where I woke up sad, stayed sad, and wanted to die. However, with a new life and a new series of changed priorities it is enough to know that I am alive because everything and anything can change with just one phone call – for good and for bad.

CHAPTER SEVENTEEN

THE GREATEST SHOWMAN

If you don't know it already, The Gypsy King, or the Big GK as I call him, is a persona. Not an alter ego, because I don't believe in them – I believe in God – but an all-singing and all-dancing character, in and out of the ring, and he's long served as an act that I will transform into when required. As I've explained in this book and elsewhere, I've often used him as a way of covering up the man beneath. For context, the real Tyson Fury is a deep thinker – though I don't like to go too deep because it can be scary sometimes. I love structure – so the Christmas holidays are the worst because every day feels like a Sunday. And I need a constant challenge; sitting around and watching TV for hours on end is not going to work for me. But The Gypsy King is a different beast all together because he is unbreakable, unshakeable, and the apex predator in his jungle.

The Gypsy King name comes from the bare-knuckle fighting scene, which is a big deal within the Traveller community. To be a King of the Gypsies is to be recognised as the best fighter of a generation, it carries some serious prestige, and my great grandfather, Othea Burton, had once held the honour, as did my distant cousin, Bartley Gorman, who was the King of the Gypsies from 1972 to 1992. So when I defeated Wladimir Klitschko, I decided to use the nickname as a way of adding to my image – my status as the world heavyweight champion gave me the authority to do so, I reckon – and it certainly captured the imagination. But it had naff-all to do with the Traveller community's fighting traditions; the title wasn't bestowed upon me, it was self-styled, and a much more memorable nickname than anything I'd toyed with in the past – *Too-Fast Fury*, *The Furious One*, and so on.

I've always known the importance of image and showmanship within the world of boxing. A glamorous, exciting or controversial fighter puts bums on seats because he creates headlines. A sense of drama often turned an average Joe into a box office sensation. Nobody was interested in the man in the corner who didn't have anything to say for himself and from what I could tell, the most famous champions were blokes who were forever dogged by controversy. They said things that upset the public (as I had) or they behaved in a way that seemed outrageous (as I did, especially when getting pissed up abroad recently). In many ways, they resembled the classic TV villain, the person you loved to hate. But nobody could match a bad boy when it came to hogging the limelight.

Take Muhammad Ali as an example: he was the youngest heavyweight to claim the title from a reigning champion at the age of twenty-two, but he was also the bloke that famously refused to fight for his country in Vietnam, which caused a right stink at the time. Prince Naseem Hamed, one of my favourite fighters ever – alongside Ricky Hatton – was a cocky so and so who winked at his opponents as he knocked them out. Everybody wanted to see him get beaten and they paid top dollar for the show. Mike Tyson, Sonny Liston, Floyd Mayweather (Jr and Sr): the sport was full of people who had run-ins with the law for one reason or another.

Sure, there have been exceptions to the rule. Frank Bruno was a quiet bloke and beloved in England, but that's because he knew how to maximise his popularity by appearing on the telly in quiz shows and adverts. When it came to show business he understood that there was more than one way to skin a cat, but that will only get someone so far. If you were to visit Azerbaijan and ask a random on the street about Frank Bruno, they'd probably shrug their shoulders and respond, '*Who?*' (No offence, Frank.) But show them a picture of Ali or Tyson and they'd identify them straightaway. I haven't wanted to be a Mr Nice Guy who was liked, but unmemorable. I have wanted to be the colourful, outspoken, charismatic and controversial entertainer.

Ultimately, that's what the boxing (and non-boxing) fan looks for too. They don't want to fork out a shedload of money for tickets and TV subscriptions only to watch boring people doing boring things. They want to feel excitement and energy, both positive and negative. That's the reason so many of us come home from work and turn on the telly to see the football, or an action film. It's escapism, we're hoping to be thrilled, and if what we're watching isn't enjoyable, we'll turn it over sharpish. I have wanted to be the person that nobody turns over, whether they want to cheer me on or boo me off.

Throughout my career I have loved being an entertainer. I have enjoyed putting on a show and doing things that other boxers wouldn't dream of, like dressing up in a sombrero and poncho for Mexican Independence weekend before my 2019 fight with Otto Wallin in Las Vegas. Or arriving at the Wembley fight in a St George's Cross robe, while being carried to the ring on a throne. I have enjoyed the passion and the cockiness, and I have loved the big TV audiences and the screaming crowds. I haven't been shy about singing a song afterwards either. (Interesting fact: when I sang 'American Pie' to 94,000 in Wembley Stadium that meant I'd played to more people at the National Stadium than bloody Ed Sheeran, and he is a bona fide pop legend.) But when you strip it all away I am a fella who makes a living by taking his shirt off in front of millions of people to fight some other massive bloke.

When I leave I think there's bound to be a void, in the same way athletics got boring once Usain Bolt had disappeared from the scene — there's no one around with the same charisma. Of course, someone will inevitably come along to fill my boots, but who knows how long that will take. I just hope we don't return to the dull old days. It was so boring when the Klitschko brothers were at the top of their game, having filled the dead zone after the era of Mike Tyson and Lennox Lewis. Other than the knockouts, it's hard to remember them doing anything vaguely exciting. Yeah, they made plenty of money out of the sport and held on to their belts for a long time, but how many times could you truly say you looked forward to one of their fights, unless they were taking on a Brit? It's just as bad now. We've been left with the Americans, some stiff Europeans, plus a bunch of boring Russians and Ukrainians. There's not a personality between them. One or two might become proper champion material, but most of the time, no one gives a toss about what they're doing.

● ● ●

There is a long line of fighters in my family. My mum came from a Traveller family who lived in Nutts Corner, near

Belfast, and her father was a King of the Gypsies. Why the Traveller community has produced so many fighters, I'm not entirely sure. Maybe it has something to do with all the persecution and prejudices we've had to deal with over the centuries. For example, my dad was bullied at school because of his background. This was the 1970s and he experienced a lot of racism, and was often getting into scraps with the kids at school. They always started it, having decided they were better than him, and my grandmother, Patience, told him to stand up for himself. Those experiences crushed people like coal; they became downtrodden, but the process turned them into diamonds, and maybe I am an example of that. I'm certainly a little rough around the edges.

Most of the men on both my mum and dad's sides either boxed or fought bare-knuckled, though nobody ever got close to my level. Back in the day, the fighters in my family were blokes trying to earn a living, though my dad was the first one who actually boxed properly at pro level. My uncle Hughie went the same way and had ten professional fights, losing around seven of them; my uncle Peter had one pro fight and lost. In the generations before them, my great-grandmother's brothers fought in World War II and were boxers in the Army. When the war ended they came out and fought in the fairgrounds for cash. None of them were dreaming of taking over the world like I did as a kid.

When I was young, the stories of my family's boxing history were fascinating, but I looked more to the likes of Muhammad Ali and Mike Tyson, Joe Louis and Lennox Lewis, Frank Bruno, Ricky Hatton and Prince Naseem Hamed. Even at a young age, I wanted to be a superstar like Sugar Ray Leonard or Marvin Hagler. I wanted the glitz and the glamour of the big fight nights in Vegas or New York; I didn't want to get my face punched in by some mediocre jack in a backyard or quarry somewhere. I wasn't even that interested in being a British champion; I wanted the world. I was aiming for the stars in order to be the best that I could. Anything less was going to be a failure.

My love of being a showman wasn't exactly signposted in my younger years because as a kid I was shy and quiet. I didn't say anything to anyone, I didn't have many mates when I was growing up and when everyone else was doing their own thing – running wild, getting drunk and doing what kids do – I was making sacrifices. I was training, so the closest I got to a gang of mates were the weights, bags and ring in the gym. If I was at some event or do in the afternoon I'd leave early because I liked to be at training by five o'clock and nothing could stop me. Boxing was all I ever wanted. I didn't need many friends. I didn't crave anything. I just wanted to box, box, box.

I was like that even after I started going out with Paris because nothing would hold me back from going to the gym. On the weekends, we would spend plenty of time together, but if I hadn't trained on those two days, the gym would be my first port of call on the Monday morning. When I later made it into the Great Britain amateur team, I was just as obsessed. I worked on my game four or five days a week, Monday to Friday. The one thing I noticed was that boxing gave me confidence. It wasn't like a switch, where I woke up one morning brimming with charisma. It was a gradual thing that gathered momentum as I realised something very important: I was good at it, better than anyone else around me at the gym, and that confidence rubbed off on my personal life.

I quickly transformed from the quiet kid who wouldn't speak to anyone, into the most outspoken bloke on the planet, like a caterpillar turning into a butterfly.

• • •

My most spectacular piece of showmanship in the ring has to be the Klitschko fight in 2015. It was the moment where I first showed the world what I was truly capable of, and after that victory, people recognised me as a fighter with the potential to upset the odds, which must have been exciting for a fan because I seemed to be the underdog in a lot of fights, especially during my second career. The fact that I clearly enjoy myself in and around a bout, no matter its importance, only adds to my appeal. I sing. I dance. I plant a smacker on my opponents — sometimes before the contest, sometimes after. And the audience, both in the arena and at home, can't take their eyes off me. I am a loose cannon and people lap it up.

I love making a grand entrance and my greatest moment of showmanship so far in that regard came recently, when I swaggered into Wembley Stadium in front of my home crowd: Kings of Leon and The Notorious B.I.G. blaring; fireworks and lightshows mesmerizing — it really doesn't get any better than that, but those moments always take a lot of planning. Before every fight I detail my walk-on to the nth degree: I know exactly what I want to wear and what I want to do as I walk through the crowd. I'll say to my team, 'Right, I'm coming out dressed as a Spartan.' Or 'This time I'm coming out in a full-on knight's outfit.' These details are then passed over to the relevant people and the magic happens from there.

I take my inspiration from all sorts of characters and events, from the fictional (Rocky Balboa) to the enigmatic (Eric Cantona). I like mavericks; I can't be doing with strait-laced people, there just isn't any entertainment value or fun in them. People that play life by the book or never get into any bother just don't interest me. There is no enjoyment in being that way either — I want to bring a sense of danger and excitement to everything I do.

Meanwhile, when it comes to the music for my grand arrivals, I have a huge playlist of songs to choose from. I love the crooners like Tom Jones; I am big into country and western and the rappers, 50 Cent (his old stuff, not the new) and Tupac Shakur. I love cuts from the twenties, thirties, forties; I enjoy soul, dance and R'n'B; I have albums from the sixties and seventies, all the way up to now. I even love musicals like *Bugsy Malone*. Once I pick out the cuts to soundtrack my entrance, I hand them over to a guy called DJ Majestic, so he can bring a mash-up together.

I also put a lot of thought into those moments of showmanship that take place away from the arena, and the most infamous of these took place in September 2015 during the build-up to the Klitschko fight. A press conference to promote our showdown was held in the build-up, and as a kid I'd always been a massive fan of the TV show, *Batman*. I even fantasised about dressing up as the Caped Crusader for an event, and like my ring walk ideas, I only needed the right stage on which to deliver it. No time seemed more perfect than in a media event preceding the biggest fight of my career, so I rocked up in a yellow Lamborghini, and kicked in the doors of the venue before running about the room. Someone even fired up the *Batman* theme tune.

'Who called for Batman?' I shouted. 'Someone called Batman!'

Klitschko didn't know what was going on. At first he applauded nervously and stared at me like I was a crazy person, but that's because I probably was at the time. Then, to add to the gag, somebody dressed as The Joker – Batman's arch-nemesis – stood up in the crowd. It was a mate I'd planted and he approached me as I took up my seat.

'Why so serious?' he yelled.

I reacted in the only way that the protector of Gotham City could: I jumped over the desk and strong-armed The Joker to the floor, knocking over Klitschko's title belts, which were being displayed at the front of the room. After rolling around with my adversary, I jumped to my feet and pointed at Klitschko.

'You are next,' I shouted. 'This is a fool, just like you are. Bloody, that's how you'll be looking when you face me on the 24 October.* You'll look up off your back you old idiot, you old fool . . .'

I then ran backstage, got dressed quickly, and rushed back to my seat at the conference, full of excuses and apologies. 'Sorry I'm late, guys,' I said. 'Got stuck in traffic . . .'

Klitschko had seen enough though. 'Tyson Fury was visiting a doctor today and he got some treatment,' he said. 'That treatment will continue until he learns how to behave

---

* This was the original date of the fight. It was postponed due to a calf injury picked up by Klitschko.

himself, respect others and become a better person. The final round of treatment will take place on the 24 October. Then, I will make him eat his words.'

Poor Klitschko hadn't fought a crazy person before and by the time I'd beaten him, he'd undoubtedly had enough of me. After our fight had ended, I grabbed the mic to sing a version of 'I Don't Want to Miss a Thing' – the hit single by Aerosmith that had become inescapable thanks to its appearance in the Hollywood blockbuster, *Armageddon*. I dedicated the song to Paris.

This is my moment, I thought. *Nobody's going to take anything away from me here . . .*

At the time, we'd spent over half our lives together and Paris had sacrificed a lot so I could live my dream as a professional fighter. I wanted to tell her that we'd conquered the world as a team. While this was going on, Klitschko waited on the side lines for his moment to be interviewed for the TV cameras.

This was yet another example of The Gypsy King persona coming to life, though as I've said, it was hard to tell him apart from the real me sometimes. I switched from the Big GK to Tyson Fury so often in those days that I sometimes struggled to tell which was which and what was what. It was a very scary place to be. There was no filter, though thanks to my recovery, I'm now at the point where I can quite comfortably switch from Tyson Fury, the man, the dad and the husband, to The Gypsy King, who everybody knows from the newspapers and the telly. When I need to be a showman, I'll turn it on like a tap. When it's vital that I behave normally, I'll do that too. These days I enjoy being me, whereas I couldn't when the boundaries were blurred. It only took me thirty-odd years of living to come to that understanding, but thank God I eventually got there. Being a showman might have killed me otherwise.

CHAPTER EIGHTEEN

NEW DAY RISING

From the minute I announced what would become a short-lived retirement after the Dillian Whyte fight in April 2022, there were calls for me to return. *Have one more fight*, they said. *Take on one last opponent.* I received so many offers that it all felt a little crazy, but I knew that if I was to take one of them up, it would have to be something special. In my mind, Dillian Whyte had seemed as good a full stop as any, especially given that everyone in my family was sick of all the drama. For them, my being a professional boxer had become a burden. But bloody hell, a comeback felt tempting. By the time you put this book down, my next fight might already be on the cards. Maybe it's happening next week, next month, or next year — *who knows?*

As far as I'm concerned, the only way I'm coming out of retirement is either for a record-breaking amount of money, or to fight in a showdown for the ages. I even told the world about the former when I announced it would take half a billion to drag me back into the ring. 'Just a quick message to let everybody know that I, The Gypsy King, am happily retired,' I said in the summer of 2022. 'But to get me out of retirement, seeing as I don't need the money, and I don't need the aggravation, it's going to cost these people half a billy, 500 million . . .'

The figure I've since been throwing around is ridiculous and deliberately so. I'm happy being retired, especially as I'm an undefeated champion, and it's all a bit of fun. But if someone's daft enough to put that type of cash on the table I'm going to have a hard think about it. *Who wouldn't?* Though the chances of it happening are slim. At one point, I was so confident that nobody was going to cough up the cash that I threw down a bet with Piers Morgan on live TV.

He said, 'How about . . . given if you do fight again, you are going to get a barrel load of cash, *gazillions*, how about if you do fight again, you have to give me a million pounds?'

I wasn't bothered. At the time I reckoned the odds of me coming back were as long as you could imagine.

'How about that's a deal?' I said.

Piers couldn't believe his luck, though I also knew that if there was a £500 million fight on the cards, I wasn't going to feel that sad about giving him a million of it. (Though he'll get it in pound coins and fivers.)

The other fight I've been interested in is a showdown to stop the nation in its tracks. A match with Anthony Joshua would fall into this category, and in September 2022, I even offered to battle him in the UK with a 60-40 split in the earnings, which surprised a lot of people. 'I'm being bombarded with messages on how much I'm going to pay

AJ,' I said. 'Everyone is saying "80-20 70-30, 75-25" – the actual answer is I've offered him 60-40.

'[That's] 40 per cent of this amazing fight because I want this fight to happen. He doesn't have any excuses now not to take it, he can't say I've low-balled him or offered him 20 per cent or 30 per cent.

'I've offered the people 40 per cent – take it or leave it, let us know.'

I made this offer because I wanted it to be a moment in sporting history, a fight for Britain. Who knows? By the time you've read this, it might even have happened.

Here's the thing with AJ: I have always been out in front of him. While I was beating Klitschko to take the world title, he was winning and retaining the international heavyweight title. In fact it was only during my hiatus that AJ was able to become the world champion. While I was having my break-down, he was always telling me to get fit, so he could fight me. But once I'd made my comeback and offered to get in the ring with him, nothing happened. Everybody knew that I was going to batter him, so I guess he didn't fancy it. I don't think he was scared of me, because boxers aren't the type to scare easily, but I do think that during the time he became the world champion – and was undefeated until 2019 – he didn't want to fight another title winner. A champion usually leaves the fights against other former champions until they're past their best, or once they've taken a load of losses.

I even remember when I was the lineal champion and Deontay Wilder was the WBC champion. With the pair of us about to fight for the first time, a former boxer said to me, 'Why are you doing it? You're both world champions, you both can make money elsewhere. Why fight each other?' But that wasn't my attitude at all. And going for it is one of the reasons why I'll be remembered long after my time's up.

Fair play though, AJ has done well. As a young man, he got himself into a bit of bother with the police but managed to turn his life around to become a world champion. As a result he's made a lot of money out of boxing, but as a fighter he's not the full ticket: AJ's always been vulnerable – he's susceptible to right hands and left hooks. Also, he's a little bit 'chinny', which means he'll win some and he'll lose some. Ultimately, I think he'll win more than he loses, but at the top level, AJ is a one-trick pony in that he's big and strong and he comes out swinging from the first round. He also throws a lot of punches. But if he hasn't knocked his opponent out within six or seven rounds, he's usually a beaten man because AJ doesn't always have the engine, or the boxing ability, to win over the distance. He's manufactured, rather than being a natural.

There is no real rivalry between us anymore, anyway. When he was the unbeaten champion there was plenty for us to get competitive about, but since his losses to Andy Ruiz Jr in 2019 and the Ukrainian Oleksandr Usyk in 2021 and 2022

I don't consider him to be on the same level. I don't even know him that well as a man and I've only met him twice. The first time was when we both appeared on *The Gloves Are Off* – that round table discussion show on Sky – alongside Lennox Lewis, Frank Bruno and Scott Welch. The second time was when we were both on holiday in Marbella at the same time. He was in the port with his pals, doing his own thing; I was heading back to wherever Paris and me were staying. We had a little chat and it was all fun. Then I said to him, 'Don't you be out here with all these idiots, drinking. Get back in the gym. Because when you lose, this lot will all have done a runner.'

I meant it too.

Given the chance, I'll take on anyone in a fight. None of them are on my level or ever will be, especially Derek Chisora, who I recently called out for a trilogy match in August 2022, having already beaten him twice. My team even offered him £2 million to do it, but in the end, the deal was turned down, so I posted a message on social media to let him know what I thought.

'I see Derek Chisora has been having a little pop; licking his wounds after losing £2 million,' I said. 'God almighty, what a mistake. *What a mistake!* You're probably going to get £375,000 for your next fight and your management team turned down £2 million. What jokers, a pack of jokers. Honestly, there's more brains in your little finger than your full management team will ever have. Where is someone like Derek Chisora going to get offered £2 million ever again?'

It's a funny thing with Chisora: we'd been pals for a while and having fought, we developed a mutual respect for one another. We even went out for dinner a couple of times, and I travelled to Monaco and Hamburg to watch him fight. But when it came to my Wembley showdown against Dillian Whyte, Chisora tipped the other bloke to knock me out. I couldn't get my head around that. How can you claim to be someone's friend and then back another fighter to send him to the canvas? I really had no idea what was eating him at the time. Perhaps it was jealousy. All I know is that I seem to be working harder than ever to put certain dossers in their place these days.

Will it ever end?

• • •

The answer, of course, is: *maybe, maybe not*. In August 2022, I travelled to Mallorca to do a meet-and-greet event known as *Fury Fest* and shortly after we arrived, the *Usyk v Joshua II* fight in Jeddah, Saudi Arabia kicked off. I didn't watch a lot of it. AJ did his best, he didn't give up and it's not like he went in there looking to lose, but afterwards he got a lot of flak for the performance. I'm not sure why. It wasn't as if Usyk was amazing. He looked to me like a tippy-tappy fighter, the sort of bloke that tries to score points by hitting at his opponent with meaningless jabs. Not a lot of judges will score those shots, especially in other boxing capitals like Vegas, where they want to see aggression, so I wasn't sure what he was trying to do.

Usyk is a new face in my division and we haven't fought so far because he isn't really from my era — it's as simple as that. He is a cruiserweight who has come into the heavy-weight class and in his first three fights he defeated the American Chazz Witherspoon in 2019, Derek Chisora in 2020, and then AJ in 2021, by which point I was planning what was supposed to be my exit from the sport against Dillian Whyte. Our stars simply haven't aligned so far and he wasn't really on my radar during the earlier stages of my second career.

Having watched him a couple of times now, I don't rate his chances against me either. In his win against Chisora, he scraped through, even though his opponent had taken nine career losses at that point. And from what I can tell, Usyk is another average European fighter — 6 foot 3 inches tall, 15 stone and pumped up with muscle. If he wasn't a south-paw, he wouldn't have as good a record as he does: 90 per cent of boxers can't fight southpaws because there aren't a lot of them about, so orthodox fighters struggle to train for their style. Sure, Usyk has beaten AJ twice now, but he's hardly a killer.

Weirdly, because of those two victories, he has built a reputation for himself as some kind of a big hitter, but I can't see that. And besides, what other cruiserweights have come up and fought at the heavyweight level and done really well? I can tell you because I'm a boxing historian: not bloody many. In fact I can only remember Tomasz Adamek, who was a good cruiserweight before turning heavyweight in 2009. He beat Chris Arreola; he beat Michael Grant; and he beat a couple of fighters that weren't very good – Vinny Maddalone and Kevin McBride. And then who did he fight? Vitali Klitschko, who absolutely punched Adamek into oblivion in 2011. The question is, can Usyk handle a proper heavyweight like me coming at him for twelve rounds?

I don't think he can.

I've been quite keen to prove it too. After the *Usyk v Joshua II* fight, I hopped onto social media, to repeat the same offer that I'd laid out earlier in the year. 'I would annihilate them on the same night. Get your chequebook out because The Gypsy King is here to stay for ever.' I set a deadline of 1 September for a response, but nothing happened.

You might be wondering, 'Well, hang on, what about those risks you were talking about earlier – the ones that made you consider retirement in the first place?' Well, fair enough. But half a billion quid is half a billion quid, and it would make anyone sit up and take notice. If the offer to come out of retirement for that amount lands next month, next year, or in a decade, I'll still take it. And sure, a purse is worthless if you die or get seriously injured in the process, but the thing is, I don't plan on doing either of those things.

If it happens, I plan on winning.

• • • •

To the big question, then: without a fight to prepare for, what can I do next, other than training and running household errands? The truth is that I'm a family man and at the moment, looking after the Furys, paying the bills and walking the dog is all I'm really interested in. Everything else is unimportant. I don't have any ambitions right now because I've done everything that I've wanted to do, and I'll be happy with whatever God gives me in the future. So let's see what he's got planned, shall we? I'm sure as time goes on, new challenges will arise. I'd quite like to run a marathon at some point, because I've done a few halves and I wouldn't mind having a shot at the real deal. There's also been some loose talk of cycling from Land's End to John O'Groats, all 874 miles of it. I want to go to the Great Wall of China and have a look at that; the pyramids in Egypt would be fun too.

More than anything I'd love to spend as much time with my family as possible. I'm very thankful that I've still got my mother and father, and my brothers and nieces and nephews. They're all so important to me, which I know is not the same for everyone. A lot of people leave home, get older and move away – some of them even move to other countries and only see their parents once or twice a year, if at all. But that wouldn't work for me. The Furys are the backbone of my life. I guess you could say we're very old-fashioned in the way we view our roots because it's where our priorities lie. I like being close to the people I love; I like being around Paris and the kids; I like hanging out with my brothers when I can. It's family first for me, and you don't go against them for anything, even if they're wrong.

We'll get together at certain points during the year, like the Christmas holidays, though as I've already told you I also like to train right through those events, because there's a weird vibe to them. For example, I make it my purpose to work on Christmas Eve, Christmas Day and Boxing Day. I'll do the same on New Year's Eve and New Year's Day because while the other dossers in my game are eating and drinking, and not training, The Gypsy King is running in the snow and getting ahead, because that's the way it has to be. I do the same thing on bank holidays and even my birthday, because I find motivation on those occasions, especially if they're events where I know other boxers will be eating themselves into oblivion with big meals, puddings, selection boxes and pies. I'll get a gang of mates together and go for a massive run instead. It gives me a sense of achievement.

I'm the same when it comes to a big night out: I want

to earn it, so if I've got a large one planned with the boys, I'll work out twice in the day and watch what I eat beforehand because I know I'm going to smash through a load of calories later that evening. This isn't a sign of my OCD at work, by the way. One of my brothers is the same. If he doesn't feel like he's earned his reward at the weekend, whether that's a night out with his family or a drink with friends, he won't bother. And if he forces himself to go, he rarely enjoys it.

Meanwhile, my brothers are a big deal to me. As well as John, Shane and Hughie, there's my two brothers Tommy and Roman – they're my dad's kids and I only met them when I was around the age of fourteen. Although I love all of them dearly, it's very rare that we get together because we're all so busy. John-Boy is a car dealer and like most people in that trade, he doesn't have a clock – he's always working hard. There's no cut-off switch. (I know that from my time in the car game.) My other two brothers, Shane and Hughie, work in landscaping and so they're up at the crack of dawn and grafting their arses off all day. But on a Friday, both of them are in the boozer at around four o'clock.

Tommy and Roman are a little bit different because they've got ambitions to be boxers. When Tommy's not training for fights, he'll be influencing on Instagram and by the looks of it, that's a job that takes him all over the world.

Sometimes I'll call him and I can tell from the ringtone that he's abroad. I'll say, 'Where are you?'

'I'm in the Seychelles.'

The Seychelles? *What the . . . ?*

'Yeah, I'm advertising some clothes, taking pictures on the beach, that kind of thing . . .'

Roman on the other hand is just starting his pro career in boxing, so he's training all the time. When he's not in the gym, slogging away for himself, he works as a personal trainer and cracks on all day, sometimes from as early as five am, right up until ten at night.

It's good to see them both following their dreams because my motto is this: *you can achieve anything in life if you really want to.* There's a big wide world out there for Roman and Tommy, John-Boy and Shane, and my six kids – *and you*, if you really want it. If your desire is to travel the planet, there's a whole world of careers in that; if you want money, there's a whole world of money; and if you want to make a big achievement in sport, business, art or science, well, there's a world of opportunity in that too. You've just got to grab the bull by the balls to get there. That takes hard work, but it's the sacrifice all of us have to make if we're to live out our ambitions. Take it from me, I know; I busted my arse to get to where I am today, and none of it would have been possible without some elbow grease and a lot of heart.

I've also realised that it's inconsequential what other people think of your dreams. As a kid, people put down my hopes whenever I talked about them, but forget them. Does it matter to the universe that I've won thirty-two fights and counting (and drawn one) throughout my unbeaten career? *Probably not*. But it matters to me, because for a long time it was my passion and my dream and it meant a lot – it certainly made a massive difference to my life. These days I can look back on my time in boxing with satisfaction, as I have done in these pages, because as a kid I knew what I wanted to be and went for it. No mucking around. Even the mistakes I made were important, because they taught me how *not* to do things. The same can happen for you, but only if you have a pop at life.

Regret's a horrible thing. I know through painful experience what it's like to rue an action I might have taken, or dwell on the way in which I have behaved – in my breakdown there were all sorts of incidents and events I would love to be able to wish away. But – cliché alert – it's far worse to regret something that you haven't done, than something you have. (And it's only a cliché because it's so true.) It's for this reason that I've hunted down my ideas and goals and not stopped until I've got my hands on them. Those targets have always been much bigger than financial security, materialism, or fame. I've wanted to prove that I am the best boxer on the planet, nothing more, and if seven billion people know of my story, or if it is a story only known to me, it won't have mattered either way. If you've spoken to a person on their deathbed and they've mentioned their regrets in life, I doubt very much they've moaned about not working enough overtime, or not buying this car, or that house. But they probably have felt bad about the person they didn't express their love for, the places they didn't visit, or the dreams they didn't chase.

You don't have to take it from me. Listen to the biblical figure Solomon, the richest person in history who, if he were alive today, would have had a net value in the trillions. At the end of his life – having been everywhere, seen everything and done it all – he stated the only things worth doing were eating, drinking and being happy in work. Other people on their deathbeds have claimed that the only truly valuable things in life were spending time with family and loved ones, and enjoying the important moments. (And I suppose those moments can vary from person to person). Apart from that, nothing else really matters.

Your job is there to pay the bills. But what you do for long-term memories is determined by the dreams you want to chase. (And if those two things cross over, well, pal, you're already winning.) That might be a life as an astronaut, a rock'n'roll star, or a sporting legend. And if you aim for the moon and fail, who cares? At least you had a right go. Because, believe me, once you've stared death in the eyes and somehow walked away in one piece, you'll have an idea of just how precious every moment on this earth is. The time is short too, so grab it by the bollocks. Because The Gypsy King did and he became the undefeated champion of his dream life.

And, trust me, he's still loving it.

MENTAL HEALTH
CONTACTS & HELPLINES

If you have been affected by mental health problems and have experienced or are experiencing suicidal thoughts, please get professional medical help immediately – contact the NHS on 111, or speak to a doctor or your GP. If you or someone you know is in danger, please contact emergency services immediately. Below is a list of mental health resources for you to explore, alongside seeking professional help.

Mind

mind.org.uk

Mind is one of the best-known UK charities devoted to helping people with mental health problems. It has around 125 local offices in England and Wales, which offer services including talking therapies, peer support, crisis care and housing support. In order to find the closest Mind to you go to: mind.org.uk/information-support/local-minds/

Anxiety Care UK

anxietycare.org.uk

Anxiety UK

03444 775774 (Monday — Friday, 9.30am — 5.30pm)
anxietyuk.org.uk

Advice and support for people living with anxiety, stress, anxiety-based depression or phobias.

British Association for Counselling and Psychotherapy (BACP)

01455 883300
bacp.co.uk

Provides information about counselling and therapy, and has a directory so you can find a therapist near you.

Improving Access to Psychological Therapies (IAPT)

nhs.uk/service-search

Use the NHS search page to find psychological therapies services near you.

The National Institute for Health and Care Excellence (NICE)

nice.org.uk

Information and clinical guidelines on recommended treatments for different conditions, including anxiety disorders.

No More Panic

nomorepanic.co.uk

Provides information, support and advice for those with panic disorder, anxiety, phobias and OCD, including a forum and chat room.

No Panic

0844 967 4848 (daily, 10am – 10pm)
nopanic.org.uk

Provides a helpline, step-by-step programmes, and support for those with anxiety disorders.

Samaritans

116 123 (24-hour service)
samaritans.org

Emotional support for anyone who needs to talk. Calls are free from all providers and do not appear on bills.

Triumph Over Phobia (TOP UK)

topuk.org

Provides self-help therapy groups and support for those with OCD, phobias and related anxiety disorders.

The Frank Bruno Foundation

thefrankbrunofoundation.co.uk

The Frank Bruno Foundation provides support, encouragement and the motivation to succeed for those facing and recovering from mental ill health.

PROFESSIONAL
BOXING RECORD

Statistics

Name	Tyson Luke Fury
Nickname(s)	Gypsy King, The Furious One, 2 Fast
Date of Birth	12 August 1988
Nationality	United Kingdom
Division	Heavyweight
Stance	Orthodox
Height	6" 9" / 206cm
Reach	85" / 216cm

Professional Fight Record

Date	Opponent	Venue	Belt	Result
23 April 2022	Dillian Whyte	Wembley Stadium, London	World Boxing Council Heavy Title *The Ring* Heavy Title	Win. Technical Knockout
9 October 2021	Deontay Wilder III	T-Mobile Arena, Paradise, Nevada	World Boxing Council Heavy Title *The Ring* Heavy Title	Win. Knockout
22 February 2020	Deontay Wilder II	MGM Grand Garden Arena, Paradise, Nevada	World Boxing Council Heavy Title *The Ring* Heavy Title	Win. Technical Knockout
14 September 2019	Otto Wallin	T-Mobile Arena, Las Vegas		Win. Unanimous Decision
15 June 2019	Tom Schwarz	MGM Grand, Las Vegas	World Boxing Organization Inter-Continental Heavy Title	Win. Technical Knockout
1 December 2018	Deontay Wilder	Staples Center, Los Angeles	World Boxing Council World Heavy Title	Draw. Split Decision
18 August 2018	Francesco Pianeta	Windsor Park, Belfast		Win. Points
9 June 2018	Sefer Seferi	Manchester Arena, Manchester		Win. Retired
28 November 2015	Wladimir Klitschko	Esprit arena, Düsseldorf	World Boxing Association Super World Heavy Title International Boxing Federation World Heavy Title World Boxing Organization World Heavy Title International Boxing Organization World Heavy Title	Win. Unanimous Decision

PROFESSIONAL BOXING RECORD

Date	Opponent	Venue	Belt	Result
28 February 2015	Christian Hammer	O2 Arena, Greenwich	World Boxing Organization International Heavy Title	Win. Retired
29 November 2014	Dereck Chisora	ExCel Arena, Dockland	World Boxing Organization International Heavy Title EBU European Heavy Title Vacant BBBofC British Heavy Title	Win. Retired
15 February 2014	Joey Abell	Copper Box Arena, Hackney Wick		Win. Technical Knockout
20 April 2013	Steve Cunningham	Madison Square Garden Theater, New York		Win. Knockout
1 December 2012	Kevin Johnson	Odyssey Arena, Belfast		Win. Unanimous Decision
7 July 2012	Vinny Maddalone	Hand Arena, Clevedon	Vacant World Boxing Organization Inter-Continental Heavy Title	Win. Technical Knockout
14 April 2012	Martin Rogan	Odyssey Arena, Belfast	Vacant BUI Ireland National Heavy Title	Win. Technical Knockout
12 November 2011	Neven Pajkić	Event City, Manchester	Commonwealth Heavy Title	Win. Technical Knockout
17 September 2011	Nicolai Firtha	Kings Hall, Belfast		Win. Technical Knockout
23 July 2011	Dereck Chisora	Wembley Arena, Wembley	Commonwealth Heavy Title BBBofC British Heavy Title	Win. Unanimous Decision

Date	Opponent	Venue	Belt	Result
19 February 2011	Marcelo Luiz Nascimento	Wembley Arena, Wembley		Win. Knockout
18 December 2010	Zack Page	Pepsi Coliseum, Quebec City		Win. Unanimous Decision
10 September 2010	Rich Power	York Hall, Bethnal Green		Win. Points
25 June 2010	John McDermott	Brentwood Centre, Brentwood	Vacant BBBofC English Heavy Title	Win. Technical Knockout
5 March 2010	Hans-Joerg Blasko	Huddersfield Sports Centre, Huddersfield		Win. Technical Knockout
26 September 2009	Tomáš Mrázek	The O2, Dublin		Win. Points
11 September 2009	John McDermott	Brentwood Centre, Brentwood	BBBofC English Heavy Title	Win. Points
18 July 2009	Aleksandrs Selezens	York Hall, Bethnal Green		Win. Technical Knockout
23 May 2009	Scott Belshaw	Colosseum, Watford		Win. Technical Knockout
11 April 2009	Mathew Ellis	York Hall, Bethnal Green		Win. Knockout
14 March 2009	Lee Swaby	Aston Events Centre, Birmingham		Win. Retired
28 February 2009	Daniil Peretyatko	Norwich Showground, Norwich		Win. Retired

Date	Opponent	Venue	Belt	Result
17 January 2009	Marcel Zeller	Robin Park Centre, Wigan		Win. Technical Knockout
6 December 2008	Béla Gyöngyösi	Nottingham Arena, Nottingham		Win. Technical Knockout

INDEX

TF indicates Tyson Fury.

Abell, Joey 101, 202–3, 299
Adamek, Tomasz 284
Adeleye, David 108
Akinwande, Henry 141, 143
Ali, Muhammad 7, 45, 124, 183, 265, 269
Amateur Boxing Association (ABA) 103, 177, 178, 181
'American Pie' (Don McLean) 266
Arreola, Chris 201, 284
Aston Events Centre, Birmingham 188, 300
Austin, Stone Cold Steve 255

Bakole, Martin 108
bare-knuckle fighting 263–4, 268
Batman 272–3
'Because I Got High' (Afroman) 244
Behind The Mask (Fury) 7, 216
Belshaw, Scott 188–9, 191, 300
Big Bear Lake training camp, San Bernardino Mountains, US 250–1
Bitcoin 145
Blasko, Hans-Joerg 193, 300

Bolt, Usain 267
Boxing Hall of Fame 5
Boxing News 124, 169
Boxing Scene 177
BoxNation 101
brain injuries 90–1
Breazeale, Dominic 38, 55
British Boxing Board of Control 28, 232, 241
British heavyweight championship 97, 110, 191, 195, 197, 198, 269
Brown, James: 'Living in America' 36
Bruno, Frank 100, 123, 155, 265, 289, 291
Burton, Othea (great-grandfather of TF) 264

Campbell, Damien 178
Cantona, Eric 271
Capetillo, Jorge 37–8
Cardiff Arms Park 123
Channel 5 110, 198
Charles, King 158
Chávez, Julio César 251

Chisora, Derek
    TF fights 101, 110, 140, 195–8,
        203, 238, 281–2, 299
    Usyk and 283–4
    Whyte and 126, 128
Christmas 107, 212–13, 263, 286
Commonwealth heavyweight
        championships 98, 110,
        177, 195, 198, 201, 299
co-promoted fights 35
Covid-19 pandemic 1, 51, 52, 53,
        62, 64, 65, 94, 101, 102
'Crazy' (Patsy Cline) 48–9
Cunningham, Steve 103, 201–2

David (biblical figure) 82–3, 84
Davison, Ben 27, 28, 31–2, 38, 40,
        235–6, 246, 252
DeGale, James 195
De La Hoya, Oscar 250
Dempsey, Jack 124
DJ Majestic 272

Egan, Jimmy 172, 173, 175, 182
Egan, Steve 173, 174–6, 177
England amateur boxing team
        74, 94, 177, 178
England football team 2, 30, 144
ESPN 35, 148, 253
Esprit Arena, Düsseldorf
        15, 207, 298
ExCel Centre, London 203, 299

50 Cent 272
Fight Night 188
Firtha, Nicolai 201, 299
Foreman, George 21, 41,
        109, 124
Fox TV 48
'Freed From Desire' (Gala) 30
Froch, Carl 47, 180
Fury, Amber (mother of TF)
        16, 71, 140–1, 159, 161, 163,
        260, 267–8
Fury, Athena (daughter of TF)
        8, 26, 59–66, 67, 76, 157
Fury Fest 282
Fury, Hugh (grandfather of TF)
        164
Fury, Hughie (brother of TF)
        157, 171, 172, 287
Fury, Hughie (cousin of TF) 229
Fury, Hughie (uncle of TF) 114,
        145–6, 195, 203–5, 214,
        216, 268
Fury, John (father of TF)
    boxing career 141–3, 268
    Styal cottage, renovation
        of 165
    TF's childhood and 158, 159,
        160, 161, 166
    TF's fights and 5, 71, 133,
        139–40, 146, 210
    TF's finances and 21–2, 62,
        147, 148, 149, 184

TF's friendships, advice on
  150, 153, 154
TF's marriage and 144–5
TF's mental health and 227
TF's name and 157
TF's second-hand car sales
  and 147, 148, 160
TF's start in boxing and 142–3,
  144, 145–6, 169, 171, 174
TF's brothers and 287
TF's training and 19, 174, 175
Traveller heritage 163, 164,
  166, 268
Fury, John-Boy (brother of TF)
  157, 169, 171, 172, 287, 288
Fury, Paris (wife of TF)
  Catholicism 73
  children and 42, 46, 59–69,
    203, 205–6, 214, 216
  fame and 75
  Gypsy background 73
  honeymoon 180–1
  Instagram workouts with TF
    51–2
  marriage to TF 74–5, 144–5, 166
  miscarriages 67, 203, 205–6,
    214, 216
  strength 75–6
  TF's fights and 16, 25, 79,
    132, 274
  TF's injuries and 15–16
  TF's lifestyle and 135, 286

TF's mental health and 8, 218,
  219, 222, 223, 228
TF's retirement and 15–16,
  25–6, 95, 96
TF's spontaneity and 57–8
TF's training and 18, 51–2,
  76–7, 269–70
Fury, Patience (grandmother of
  TF) 162, 268
Fury, Peter (uncle of TF) 145–6,
  208, 268
Fury, Prince Adonis Amaziah
  (son of TF) 63, 64, 70
Fury, Prince Tyson (son of TF)
  63, 70
Fury, Roman (brother of TF)
  287, 288
Fury, Shane (brother of TF) 90,
  142, 157, 161, 171, 172, 182,
  287, 288, 289
Fury, Tommy (brother of TF)
  133, 287, 288
Fury II, Prince John James (son
  of TF) 43, 63, 69, 70
Fury, Tyson
  alcohol and 8, 27, 91, 118, 119–20,
    133–4, 136, 145, 218, 219–20,
    221, 223, 226, 231, 287
  amateur boxing career 24, 68,
    74, 94, 98, 103, 175, 176–9,
    181, 183–4, 205, 213, 270
  ambition 143

Fury, Tyson (*cont'd*)

America, elevated status in 34–5, 253–7

ankle injuries 144, 223, 229

anxiety 8, 79, 88, 117, 159, 206, 226, 237

baldness 243–4

bipolar 8

birth 157

bone spurs 108–9

boxing, first takes up 171–5

boxing licence revoked by British Boxing Board of Control 28, 232, 238–9, 241

brain-injuries and 90–1

bullies and 166–7

caravan lifestyle and 165–6

cars 8, 23, 184–5, 225, 254

Catholicism 45, 73, 82–3, 164–5, 231

chicken breeding and trading 161

childhood 23, 155–62, 169–70, 223, 246, 247

children and. *See individual child name*

Christmas and 107, 212–13, 263, 286

coaches. *See individual coach name*

cocaine consumption 8, 28, 221

combination punching 32, 129, 174, 211

comeback (2018) 15, 27–51, 93–4, 101, 112, 127, 140, 225, 231–4, 235–47

confidence 28, 45, 47, 104, 122–3, 156, 176, 255, 270

costumes 36, 47–8, 102, 207, 266, 271

cuts 37–8

cycling 285

daily routine 19, 217–18

depression 7, 8, 19, 29, 50, 107, 134–5, 159, 206, 214, 215, 218, 219, 223, 225, 237, 247, 258, 260

desire to win 82–3

diet 7–8, 17, 27, 111–12, 113, 182–3, 189–90, 217

drug-taking 8, 28, 145, 221, 229

entertainer/showmanship 7, 48, 127, 183, 202, 216–17, 254, 257, 263–75

entourage 152

ESPN TV deal 35, 148, 253

exercise, importance of to 52, 113, 136, 252, 258–60

fame 14, 71–2, 75, 146, 149, 150, 151, 183, 214

family and 59–77. *See also individual family member name*

fear and 18–20, 67, 81, 82, 122

fighters in family of 267–8

fights, first competitive 169–72, 176. *See also individual opponent name*

fights, first professional 181–2. *See also individual opponent name*

finances 21–3, 24, 72, 91, 94, 98, 147, 149–50, 153, 160, 161, 174, 175, 179, 184–5, 190, 196, 201–2, 213, 214, 221, 224, 233, 239, 242, 277, 278, 279, 280, 289

footwork 41, 109, 173, 209, 211

foreign soil, contest on 31, 34

friendship, on importance of 150–4

gloves 209

Gypsy background 73

Gypsy King nickname 47, 48

Gypsy King persona 263–75

haters and 27, 143

heart rate monitors and 116

height 4, 172, 197, 198, 208

honeymoon 180–1

ice baths and 115

information, thirst for 123–4

injuries 15–16, 57, 90–1, 108–9, 144, 223, 229, 257

Irish Traveller heritage 48, 73, 74, 147, 162–8, 225, 263, 264, 267–8

karaoke 44

'kidnapped' by father, brother and cousin 19

Las Vegas, buys house in 253

legacy 9, 14, 207

letters written to 34

manual labourer 148–9

marathon, ambition to run a 285

mavericks, admires 271

meet-and-greet tour 66–7

mental breakdown 8, 27, 72, 136, 212–34 239, 242, 244, 279–80, 289

mental health 6, 7, 8, 27, 28, 29, 34, 48, 52, 72, 76, 79, 80, 107, 134, 136, 193, 206, 212, 212–34, 237, 238, 239, 242, 244, 258, 261, 279–80, 291. *See also individual mental health issue*

mental strength 85–8

music and. *See individual artist or song name*

nandrolone levels 229, 241

obsessive compulsive disorder (OCD) 8, 88, 117, 206, 287

Fury, Tyson (*cont'd*)
　　opponent research 125
　　opponent standards and
　　　　125–6
　　orthodox fighter 129, 173, 210,
　　　　212, 283
　　panic attacks 224
　　pantomime villain 216–17
　　Paradise Syndrome and
　　　　213–14, 259
　　paranoia 8
　　patience, lack of 118
　　perfectionist 117
　　pre-match routines 4–6
　　press/media and 2, 5, 75, 80,
　　　　183, 217
　　press conferences 19, 29, 56,
　　　　61, 81, 82, 102, 120, 121–2,
　　　　183, 197, 207, 215, 222,
　　　　229–30, 244, 272
　　professional, turns 75, 103, 177,
　　　　179, 181, 183–5, 187
　　punches, five main 129
　　psychiatrist, sees 226–30, 231,
　　　　232, 241
　　reading 123–5
　　recluse 135
　　red zone, training in 116, 117
　　retirement 3, 7, 9, 13–15, 18,
　　　　20–1, 24, 25–6, 52, 93, 94,
　　　　95, 96, 133, 223, 231–2, 234,
　　　　277–85

ring design and 209
ring entrances 1–3, 30, 47–9,
　　256, 271, 272
ring walk 36, 47, 48, 272
school 147, 158
scrap dealing 160, 161–2
selfish nature of boxing
　　profession and 16–18
second-hand car salesman 9,
　　102, 147, 148, 160, 183–4,
　　288
short-term memory loss 9
southpaws and 173
sparring 45, 98–9, 108, 113, 115,
　　116, 127, 155, 172, 176, 217,
　　236
spontaneity 57–8, 260–1
straight punch 41
suicidal thoughts 8, 224–6, 259
suicide attempt 8, 224–6,
　　228–9, 245, 259
support team 111
tennis elbow 109
timing 130–1
Top Rank deal 35, 253
training 1, 2, 5, 17–18, 19, 27–8,
　　40–7, 51–2, 65–6, 71, 88,
　　94, 97, 104, 107, 125, 135,
　　141, 142, 143, 145–6, 151,
　　169, 172, 173, 175, 179, 180,
　　182, 189, 190, 193, 208, 222,
　　231, 235–6, 247, 256, 259,

260, 269, 270, 284, 285, 287, 288

camps 17, 18, 40, 44, 45, 48, 52, 61, 76–7, 86, 98–9, 105, 107–20, 139, 152, 201–2, 214, 215, 225, 235–6, 250–4

group 98

gyms. *See individual gym name*

importance of 52, 113, 136, 252, 259–60

live on Instagram 51–2

trainers. *See individual trainer name*

United Kingdom Anti-Doping (UKAD) charge 229, 241

unusual boxing style 110

US debut 201–2

weigh-ins 80, 208, 244, 257

weight 8, 26–8, 39, 66, 112, 116, 172, 176, 182, 189–90, 206, 208, 218, 222, 232, 233, 235, 236, 238, 252

wife. *See Fury, Paris*

work ethic 71, 147, 162, 175

work-life balance 119

WWE and 255–8

Fury, Valencia Amber (daughter of TF) 63–4, 70

Fury, Venezuela (daughter of TF) 42, 63–4, 69, 70

Gavin, Frankie 196

Glazkov, Vyacheslav 220

Gloves Are Off, The (TV show) 155–6, 185, 281

Gorman, Bartley (cousin of TF) 264

Grant, Michael 284

Great Britain amateur boxing team 74, 141, 178, 270

Groves, George 195

Guinness Book of World Records 125

Gyongyosi, Bela 47, 180, 181–2, 184, 187, 301

Hagler, Marvin 269

Hakkasan nightclub, Las Vegas 91

Hamed, Prince Naseem 45, 183, 265, 269

Hammer, Christian 203, 229, 299

Hart, Bret 'The Hitman' 255

Hatton, Ricky 65, 72, 100, 246, 265, 269

Haye, David 206

Hearns, Thomas 40

heart rate monitors 116

Hennessy, Mick 180, 230–1

Hollywood 22, 50, 155, 251, 274

Holmes, Larry 21

ice baths 115

'I Don't Want to Miss A Thing' (Aerosmith) 274

'I'm Gonna Have a Little Talk
    With Jesus' (Randy
    Travis) 20
Instagram 51–2, 287
inter-continental heavyweight
    championship 97, 196,
    298, 299
International Boxing Federation
    (IBF) 15, 36, 121, 193,
    212, 219–20
International Boxing
    Organisation (IBO) 15,
    193, 212, 230
Ireland amateur boxing team 177
Irish heavyweight
    championship 97, 110
Irish Travellers 48, 73, 74, 147,
    162–8, 228, 263–4, 267–8
Isley Brothers, The: 'It's Your
    Thing' 256
ITV 182, 188–9

Janson, Marshall 139
Jeffries, James J. 124
Jesus Christ 20, 81, 136, 153
Jimmy Egan Boxing Academy,
    Wythenshawe 172–6, 182
Johnson, Kevin 201, 299
Jones, Tom 272
Joshua, Anthony 28, 254
    childhood 155–6
    KOs 126

Martin fight 121
Ruiz fights 116, 121
TF fight with, proposed
    278–81
Usyk fights 121, 280–1, 282–4
Whyte fight 97, 128
Wilder and 233–4
Jubilee Tower, Lancaster
    27–8
'Juicy' (Notorious B.I.G.) 2

Khan, Amir 100, 251
King, Don 169
Klitschko, Vitali 201,
    209–10, 284
Klitschko, Wladimir 244, 254,
    256, 267
    Chisora and 195
    Fury v Klitschko I (2015) 7, 14–15,
    35, 80, 102, 116, 121, 128,
    139, 183, 193–4, 195, 198–9,
    201–17, 221, 237, 264,
    270–1, 272–4, 279, 298
    Fury v Klitschko II (cancelled)
    28, 217, 220, 222–3, 224,
    229–30, 238–9, 241
    killer instinct 84
    'Manny' Steward and 40,
    45, 70
    TF joins training camp of 40
Kronk Gym, Detroit 40, 43,
    44, 45

Lee, Duncan 176
Leonard, Sugar Ray 269
Lewis, Lennox 21, 35, 40, 123, 155,
    170, 218, 250, 267, 269, 281
Liston, Sonny 265
Louis, Joe 269
Lowe, Isaac 151

Maddalone, Vinny 201, 284, 299
Madison Square Garden, New
    York 95–6, 103, 201–2, 299
'Mama Said Knock You Out'
    (LL Cool J) 244
Manchester Arena 222, 229, 241,
    298
Manchester United 70, 104, 158
Marciano, Rocky 93
Martin, Charles 121
Matrix, The 36
Mayweather Jr, Floyd 265
Mayweather Sr, Floyd 265
McBride, Kevin 284
McDermott, John 190–1,
    192, 193, 300
McGregor, Conor 111
McKenzie, Duke 188–9
MGM Grand Garden Arena,
    Vegas 38, 298
Miller, Jarrell 108
Morecambe Football Club 65, 76
Morgan, Piers 170, 278
Mosley, Shane 251

Motown 44
Mutley, Young 196

nandrolone 229, 241
Nascimento, Marcelo Luiz
    140, 300
Nelson, Johnny 209
Netflix 148, 162
Nottingham Arena 180, 301
nutrition 7–8, 17, 111–12, 182–3

Oasis 128
Old Trafford 103
Olympic Games 177
    (1998) 141
    (2008) 178
O'Neal, Shaquille 69
Ortiz, Luis 38, 250
O2 Arena 128, 195, 203, 299

Pacquiao, Manny 251
Page, Zack 46, 193, 300
Pajkić, Nevan 201, 299
Paradise Syndrome 213–14, 259
Parker, Joseph 151
Pascal, Jean 47, 180
Pianeta, Francesco 28, 93–4, 100,
    245, 247, 249, 252, 298
Povetkin, Alexander 97
Power, Rich 193, 300
Price, David 177–8
Priory, The 247

promoters, boxing 22–3, 25, 29,
31, 35, 38, 93, 100, 101,
102, 121, 146, 171, 180, 184,
193, 195–6, 219, 241, 249,
253. *See also individual
promoter name*

Range Rover Sport 184–5
red zone 116, 117
Reid, Pelé 191
'Return of The Mack' (Mark
Morrison) 244
Ring, The 15, 212, 298
Rivas, Oscar 128
Roach, Freddie 251
Rock, The 255
Rocky films 36, 155, 194, 271
Rocky IV 194
Rolling Stone 230, 238
Rolls-Royce 23, 184, 254
Ronaldo, Cristiano 104–5
Ruiz Jr, Andy 116, 280

Sanchez, Abel 250
Saunders, Billy Joe 235
Schwarz, Tom 35–7, 126, 255, 298
Seferi, Sefer 28, 100, 241–5, 247,
249, 252, 298
'Sex on Fire' (Kings of Leon)
2, 271
Shakur, Tupac 272
Shaw, Gary 184

Sheeran, Ed 151–2, 266
Sky Sports 155, 209
social media 55, 71, 79, 232, 235,
249, 281, 284
Solomon 290–1
Sporting News, The 258
sports science 116–17, 194
Staples Center, Los Angeles
28–9, 30, 95–6, 103–4,
250, 298
Steve Egan Boxing
Academy 177
Steward, Emanuel 'Manny' 5, 40,
42–7, 194, 197, 250
Steward, SugarHill 151
first invited into Fury camp
40–4
Fury v Wilder II and 40–4, 46,
47, 49, 61, 84–5
Fury v Wilder III and 107–8, 111
Fury v Whyte and 5, 128, 129,
132, 133–4, 136
Stiverne, Bermane 201, 250
Strowman, Braun 255, 256–7
Styal 157–8, 159, 165
Sulaimán, Mauricio 96
Swaby, Lee 188, 191, 300

Team GB 178
'Ten Crack Commandments'
(The Notorious B.I.G.)
145–6

T-Mobile Arena, Vegas 52, 298
Top Rank 35, 253
Tyson, Mike 35, 126, 157, 183, 218, 233, 265, 267, 269

United Kingdom Anti-Doping (UKAD) 229, 241
Usyk, Oleksandr 121, 280–1, 282–4

Wallin, Otto 35, 37–8, 126, 253, 255, 266, 298
Warren, Frank 25, 29, 93, 100–2, 121, 146, 171, 196, 241, 249–50
Washington, Gerald 250
Welch, Scott 155–6, 185, 281
Wembley Stadium 1–6, 93, 95, 96–8, 99, 100, 101, 102–3, 104, 110, 121, 123, 126, 127, 128, 133, 134, 139, 140, 259, 266, 271, 282, 298, 299, 300
Whyte, Dillian 1–6, 97–105, 109, 121–32, 135, 139, 144, 259, 277, 282, 284, 298
Wilder, Deontay 97, 118, 140, 144, 212, 280
    Fury v Wilder I (2018) 26–34, 35, 80, 96, 104, 146, 232–3, 235, 240, 249–53, 298

Fury v Wilder II (2020) 35, 38, 39–51, 53–5, 80, 96, 111, 126, 253, 255, 257–9, 298
Fury v Wilder III (2021) 8, 9, 25–6, 52, 52–8, 59, 61, 62, 64, 66, 76–7, 80–91, 93, 96, 107, 110, 126, 146, 259, 298
Williams, Robbie 212–13, 259
Witherspoon, Chazz 283
'Without Me' (Eminem) 244
World Boxing Association (WBA) 15, 212, 230
World Boxing Council (WBC) 26, 96, 97, 201, 212, 250, 258, 260
World Boxing Organisation (WBO)
    heavyweight championships 15, 97, 98, 141, 151, 193, 194, 195, 203, 212, 230, 235, 236
    inter-continental welterweight title 196
World Wrestling Entertainment (WWE) 255–7

York Hall, Bethnal Green 103, 178, 300

Zeller, Marcel 187–8, 191, 301

LIST OF ILLUSTRATIONS

Plate Section 1

p.1 Top: © Warren Little / Getty. Middle: © Mikey Williams / Getty. Bottom: © Peter Cziborra / Alamy.

p. 2 Top: © John Walton / Alamy. Bottom left: © PxlImages / Alamy. Bottom right: © ZUMA Press / Alamy.

p. 3 Top: © Julian Finney / Getty. Bottom left: © Peter Cziborra / Alamy. Bottom right: © Julian Finney / Getty.

p. 4 Top: © Peter Cziborra / Alamy. Upper middle: © Andrew Coulridge / Alamy. Lower middle: © Nick Potts / Alamy. Bottom: © Andrew Coulridge / Alamy.

p. 5 Top: © Everett Collection / Alamy. Bottom: © JPA / AFF-USA / Alamy.

p. 6 Top: © MB Media / Getty. Bottom: © Al Bello / Getty.

p. 7 Top: © UPI / Alamy. Bottom: © Al Bello / Getty.

p. 8 Both images: © Al Bello / Getty.

Plate Section 2

p.1 All images: © Paris Fury.

p. 2 Top: © Reuters / Alamy. Bottom two: © ITV.

p. 3 Top & bottom images: © Tyson Fury. Right: © Tommy Fury.

p. 4 Both images: © Paris Fury.

p. 5 Both images: © Paris Fury.

p. 6 Top: © John Fury. All others © Tyson Fury.

p. 7 Top: © SugarHill Steward. Bottom: © Kristian Blacklock.

p. 8 All images: © Tyson Fury.

Plate Section 3

p.1 Top: © David Ashdown / Alamy. Bottom: © Jason Cairnduff / Alamy.

p. 2 Top two: © TGSPHOTO / Alamy. Bottom two: © Peter Cziborra / Alamy.

p. 3 Top two: © Nick Potts / Alamy. Middle left: © Kai Pfaffenbach / Alamy. Middle right: © DPA / Alamy. Bottom left: © Ina Fassbender / Alamy.

p. 4 Top: © ZUMA Press / Alamy. Bottom: © Lionel Hahn / Alamy.

p. 5 Top: © ZUMA Press / Alamy. Middle two: © Isaac Brekken / Alamy. Bottom left: © USA TODAY Network / Alamy. Bottom right: © Bradley Collyer / Alamy.

p. 6 Top: © Paul Currie/ BPI / Shutterstock. Middle Left: © Tyson Fury. Middle right: © ZUMA Press / Alamy. Bottom: © Zuma Press, Inc. / Alamy.